FROM NU

Clare Richards lives in Norwich with her husband and two children. Trained as a teacher, she was for fourteen years a nun. In 1980 she and her husband adopted twin babies born in a remote village in the Andes. In recent years she has returned to teaching part-time, as well as writing books for schools.

FROM NUN TO MUM

Clare Richards

Tri△NGlE

First published 1991
Triangle
SPCK
Holy Trinity Church
Marylebone Road
London NW1 4DU

British Library Cataloguing in Publication Data
Richards, Clare
From nun to mum: an ex-nun adopts twins from South America.
1. Catholic church. Nuns – Biographies
I. Title
271.9002

ISBN 0-281-04509-7

Typeset by Inforum Typesetting, Portsmouth
Printed in Great Britain by
BPCC Hazell Books
Aylesbury, Bucks
Member of BPCC Ltd

This book is for
all the nuns
friends
and members of my family
who form part of this story
but especially for
Georgette
who is all three

Contents

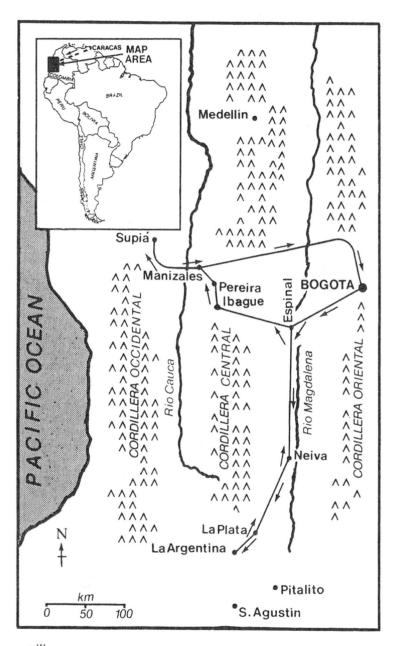

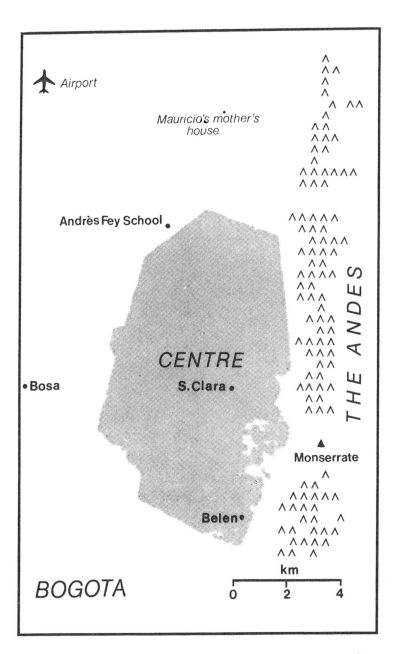

Airport

Mauricio's mother's house

Andrès Fey School

CENTRE

Bosa

S. Clara

THE ANDES

Monserrate

Belen

km

0   2   4

BOGOTA

List of Photographs

Between pp 48 and 49

All the photos of Colombia are courtesy of BBC tv East, taken by
Linda Hutchings, Alan Neale and Roy Williamson.

Introduction

It is 6.00 am. I've hardly slept at all. There is a haunting stillness about this place. A quietness which is broken by unfamiliar night sounds; horses galloping up the narrow street outside our shuttered window; the cock crowing hourly through the night; bursts of singing and guitar music from open doorways. And there is the soft breathing of my daughter at my side, and the occasional snoring from her father in rhythm with the gentler nasal breathing of our son.

We are here together, sleeping in one simple room, in a house deep in the Andes mountains. We arrived yesterday. For the last three hours we had jolted along a winding potholed dirt-track through the rich green slopes of Colombia's coffee and cotton valleys. We rounded a final twist in the track and our small village, La Argentina, lay below us. The evening sun had settled over the valley and we gasped at the beauty of the place.

Ten minutes later as we snaked our way towards the village a rainbow silently arched across the clouds and enclosed the houses in its curve. It was the first time I had ever seen both ends of a rainbow, sharp and beautiful, mysteriously tipping the trees. The village was completely enclosed in the halo of colours. It was an unforgettable moment. The BBC team accompanying us on our journey leapt from the van to capture the picture. I'm glad we will have a permanent reminder of the extraordinary timing of the event.

La Argentina is waking up. More shouts. More horses' hooves on the dusty road. Shutters banging and distant guitar music in Spanish rhythm. Moths are flitting around the light in the hallway and the smell of coffee tells me it is time to get up.

I don't know what the day will bring.

We've dreamt about this day, planned it and worried about it. For nine years we have been preparing our children for it. I sense it is going to be special.

And one thing has resolved itself in my mind during the night. I am going to write down the story of this remarkable journey.

In August 1980 my husband and I travelled to Colombia to adopt our twins, Pedro and Blanca. We were an unlikely couple to start a family. Bert had been a Roman Catholic priest and I had been a nun for nearly fourteen years. It was the nuns of my former Congregation who had helped us to find our much wanted children.

In August 1989 Bert and I took Blanca and Pedro back to Colombia for the 'journey of a lifetime'. We had always wanted them to know their Andean village and to 'feel' the warmth and love of their own Indian people. The BBC decided to accompany us, to record this return to roots, for an Everyman programme. Overseas adoptions are of controversial concern in this country and the programme met with enormous interest. A year later we are still receiving letters from all over Britain.

By August 1990 I had given my seventieth talk entitled 'From Nun to Mum'. I discovered that people were very interested in the other journey I took, the journey from one lifestyle to another. Group after group in the village and church halls of Norfolk have asked me to write down the whole story.

So here it is. Every holiday our family write a diary. I

start each of the chapters with an extract from the 1989 return trip diary. These extracts allow me to look back over the past and retrace the steps of my life journey. In doing so I have tried to analyse my shift in interpretation of Roman Catholic values. For it was this that led me to swap the life of a nun for the life of a happily married wife and mother.

1 THE NUNS

DIARY August 1

There is preparation and preparation.

Long term, it dates back years, when we opened a bank account called 'Neiva' and salted away £30 per month to finance this trip.

Shorter term, the whole of July, it seemed we went shopping daily for clothes and shoes and presents and knick-knacks to kit ourselves out. Not to mention dozens of inoculations.

Shorter still, the whole spare bedroom festooned with the packing, and the sad conclusion that our cases were too inadequate; so we went to the sales to buy some more.

The immediate preparation was all yesterday morning, when the front room became a wilderness of packing, and the rest of the house a desert of moaning hoovers and dusting. Visitors were not deterred, and arrived in droves to wish us well (one stayed for two hours!) distracting us from the exacting task. (Did I pack those pills? in which case? What happened to those canvas shoes? Who's got Blanca's koala?)

The chaos finally solved itself. It always does, and we were off by 1 pm. At Celia's by 3.45 for tea and freshly baked *apfeltorte*. An easy journey in her car to Heathrow, farewells, and the problem-free check in with VIASA. The BBC filmed us and got some good shots. Lots of time for duty-free, no delay for embarking on our DC10 (our eyebrows corrugated — there have been two DC10 crashes last month), and off on time and in a half empty cabin to Frankfurt where we picked up more sun-seekers.

Generous snacks and drinks followed by dinner about 2 am.

A film was shown overnight but it didn't seem worth staying awake for. We slept fitfully. Amusing to see the BBC wake up Bert in order to film him sleeping. 8.30 am London time we landed smoothly at Caracas in Venezuela. A deadly three-hour wait which turned out to be four, and we eventually boarded a plane for the hour's journey to Bogota, enlivened by a second breakfast of scrambled eggs, a thick slice of bacon, fried potatoes, fruit, orange juice and coffee.

Journeys. That's what I'm writing about. Not just this South American saga, but the long journey which saw me enter a convent, leave it again, get married and have a family. It's the long journey from nun to mum.

I wouldn't be surprised if the journey started as long ago as my first visit to a convent. My first encounter with a nun frightened me. I was four years old and had been taken by my parents to visit the local convent school where I was to become a pupil. Three or four voluminous black shapes descended upon us and isolated me from my mother. All I could see as I looked up was black. I had been told that the nuns were kind ladies and I did so want to start school. But for a moment I doubted the wisdom of it. These dark shapes reminded me of my fairy story 'baddies'. They looked more like witches than fairy godmothers. My mother pushed her way back to my side as Sister Cyril spoke to me, and just in time my courage returned.

I grew to like Sister Cyril very much. Her musical French accent and her warm smile made her very attractive. She had a gracious walk and an air of calm which made her always a little mysterious. She is, I think, still alive. I met her some years ago and she seemed not to have changed. I have no doubt that her bearing still makes her a carbon copy of most people's idea of the Roman Catholic nun — just a little remote, peaceful, holy and safely insulated from the temptations of a materialistic world. I also have no doubt that she herself would smile at such a simplistic view.

For six years my sister and I walked the daily mile to and from the private convent school. It would have been more convenient and cost nothing if we had gone with the local children to the primary school round the corner. As it was my parents wanted to keep to the promise they had made at their marriage to give their children a Catholic education. It was a mixed marriage. My mother is a Catholic, my father isn't. Catholic Church law demanded that my father accept all the commands of Catholic discipline. An Englishman's word is his bond, they say. My father is every inch an Englishman. To educate us in this way was a sacrifice. I never recall Mum and Dad having money to spend on themselves. Every penny of Dad's very moderate wage was accounted for. And school fees took a disproportionate bit out of his earnings. Later my mother had to go back to work to pay for our secondary education.

How is it that some people can recall sitting in their prams? I have only the vaguest memories of my early years at the convent. I know I loved school from the word go. But the clearest memories that I have of those days are unpleasant ones. I was about six years old when I inherited a rather sharp and often impatient teacher, Miss O'Regan. One day she asked us to write down the initials of our full name. I wrote down PAM. They were my initials — Pamela Alice Milward. 'I did NOT tell you to write your Christian name,' she shouted at me with great irritation. In vain I tried to tell her my full name. But she wouldn't listen. I felt very grieved and I was never at ease with her again. It cast a shadow over the rest of that school year.

My first encounter with a Mother Superior was also not a happy one. Our school was made up of a number of large detached houses set in fine grounds. Lawns and orchards bordered the playgrounds. I think I had left Miss O'Regan's class when the apple incident took place. A group of us were playing ball when it strayed into the apple orchard. The grass was strewn with windfalls. The temptation was too great. Jennifer and I took an apple and were stealthily eating into them when Sister Regina bore down on us. Her horror at our 'stealing' the forbidden fruit was absolute. We got the ultimate punishment. We were sent to report our misdemeanour to Reverend Mother herself, an awesome figure only seen at prize day, once a year. I can still recall a dreadful sense of fear as, in deepest disgrace, Jennifer and I crossed the road outside the school and walked down to the convent. I don't think we were scolded overmuch but I felt a sense of guilt which lasted for a very long time.

Three big events coloured my seventh year. I made my first communion, I went to my first football match and my brother was born. I don't pretend to any spiritual enlightenment on that first communion day. Like most seven-year-olds my mind was really only on the beautiful white dress and veil that I was wearing. Unwittingly my godmother caused me a great disappointment on the day itself, which we had been told was going to be the happiest in our whole life. Auntie Madge lent me the luxurious white covered prayer book she had carried at her wedding. This meant that when all of the other children were given a new communion prayer book to celebrate the occasion, I wasn't. They all took theirs home. I had to return mine to my aunt. It rather spoilt the day.

My first football match was to have a lasting effect on me. Dad went to see Barnet play every week, and I was intrigued when he announced that they were going to play a team from China. I went with him out of curiosity. I was hooked. For the next eleven years I never missed a match. The Barnet and Tottenham players were my heroes. Within a few years I was so much part of the football scene that I used to wash and darn the team's socks.

Richard was born in the front bedroom in the early hours of a spring morning. I can vividly recall the hushed whispers my sister Georgette and I exchanged as we pretended to be sleeping through the happy drama. Dad stayed downstairs holding his breath; we too could hardly breathe with excitement. When the midwife shouted down the stairs, 'You have a son', and the little gasping cries of the newborn brother reached us, we were out of bed and by our door even before Dad, taking the stairs two at a time, could reach our mother to admire her achievement.

Richard was a lovely baby and arrived at a clever time. With sisters aged seven and nine he could hardly go wrong. We adored him, and being enthusiastic Brownie age, we must have been a godsend to Mum. We washed him, entertained him, rocked him, and later fed him.

All my memories of home life are secure and comfortable ones. On reflection I realise now that by sheer instinct my parents played the parenting role exactly as Doctor Jolly or Penelope Leach would later approve. When the custom of the day was to let a baby cry, Mum and Dad would pick us up and soothe us to sleep. My father was always firm but never hard on us. We knew where we were and what he expected of us. My earliest memory of Dad is of sitting on his knee learning to read.

He later even taught me how to knit! Then there were the hours spent with him on his allotment. I only have to think of them to taste new peas all over again. Not cooked peas but the small sweet ones which we unpodded, sitting on the garden step on Sunday mornings. Dad was a good DIY man, a perfectionist in fact. This meant standing for what seemed like hours holding pieces of wood for him. Poor Mum seemed to be stepping round us all the time as the operation usually took place in the kitchen.

When I think of my mother during these growing up days, I can only remember spending most of our time talking and laughing together. My older sister was far more practical than me. It was she who did the tidying up and later made shopping lists and got on with things. Mum and I could get distracted even over making a cup of tea. We would be laughing over some silly incident we had witnessed and nattering nineteen to the dozen when voices would call from the sitting room, 'Is that tea *ever* going to come?' My father must have said a thousand times, 'What *do* you two find to talk about?' I have to admit that we have never really stopped talking. If I get on the phone to Mum even now, we will probably be trying to put the world right or choosing the England team for the World Cup.

Childhood days for me are Saturday football, Sunday picnics with games of French cricket, (how is it that the sun was always shining and that I have never since tasted tomatoes like Dad's home-grown ones?) and the annual holiday by the sea with me always acting as navigator in the front seat next to Dad. They are days of contentment with very little in the way of new toys, new clothes and new entertainments. What we lacked in material possessions we gained through the love and ingenuity of our parents. Both Mum and Dad had had tough childhoods. They were deprived of almost everything. Dad had to leave school at twelve to provide for his widowed mother, and Mum had to abandon her grammar school education at fifteen although she had the potential of becoming a star pupil. They had resolved to give us all the opportunities they never had. And to their eternal credit I have never once heard them complain that we could do things that they had never been able to do.

2 SCHOOL

DIARY August 2

Our first night in Bogota was a strain. We were guests in a pleasant house in the posh northern suburbs (a guard keeps a chain across the road, and parades up and down with a gun). Doors are all double doors, all with double locks. With gracious good intentions Mauricio — whom we had known as a student in Norwich — insisted we stay with his mother. But things got us down a bit last night:

(a) The difficulty of being in a house where only Spanish is spoken.

(b) The sense of being involuntary prisoners, miles from town, when we had planned an independent hotel life in the centre.

(c) The altitude of Bogota, which makes breathing laboured and gives chest pains and wooziness at every expanded effort.

By 8.00 pm (1.00 am our time) we longed to escape but were still being regaled by relatives about business prospects, and about how awful Miami had become since it had been swamped with refugees from Nicaragua. Not our scene at all. We await better things in the morning when the jetlag will presumably be less, and we meet the sisters who first cared for Pedro and Blanca.

Sunday morning. First stop Colegio Santa Clara, the fee-paying girls' prep and grammar school in the heart of the city, run by the Sisters of the Poor Child Jesus. The welcome by the new superior, Rosa Emilia, could not have been warmer. Today was open day and yet she insisted on coming out to fetch us, despite hundreds of rich parents demanding attention.

At S. Clara chaos. The families had gathered and there was hubbub everywhere, not least in the sunny garden where there was a dancing display by fifty tots. From the melée emerged one nun after another to greet us. Nine years almost to the day when we had first arrived here to adopt Pedro and Blanca.

Mass in the crowded school chapel with girls, families, nuns and novices. Lively guitar music and choir, reminding us of that Mass years ago when the girls read out a bidding prayer asking for blessings on the Richards family.

Met the loquacious over 80-year-old Sr Virgilia who typically countered our German greeting with, 'Why you speaking me German? I speak English perfect. I am in Finchley', and then turned to another visitor claiming her attention with, 'You speak with me Dutch?' She was ever thus, but is clearly on her way to telling her life story to the Holy Spirit.

An enormous lunch in the parlour. Then off to visit the infirmary where we had first taken full-time charge of our children (traumatic memories). Everywhere we went the nuns exclaimed, 'Miracle, miracle' when they saw Pedro and Blanca so full of life, so charming and playful. They seem to be coping with jetlag better than us. Later Rosa Emilia insisted on leaving the throng to take us back via a Sunday Superstore to buy necessary postcards, a cigarette lighter and tonic for our duty-free gin.

Colegio Santa Clara has a strange effect on me. I have a sense of homecoming here. Everything about it is familiar and comfortable. It is the Bogota equivalent of my own convent school — St Michael's in Finchley, London, which was also run by the Sisters of the Poor Child Jesus. (Both were originally founded by the Congregation to finance the work amongst the poor. The Bogota school continues to do this. The welfare state in England has made this unnecessary for the English school).

I left the French convent and moved to St Michael's when I was ten. My sister Georgette had gone the year before but failed to get a scholarship place. It was thought I might have a better chance of passing the eleven-plus if I was already in the St Michael's prep school, but I failed the exam too. When it came to his turn, my brother didn't pass the scholarship either. Today he is a highly successful accountant, Georgette is a headmistress and I am a teacher. So much for testing academic ability at eleven!

Thank goodness the nuns were generous. Otherwise our convent days would have been ended; there was no way my parents could pay fees for all three of us. On the sisters' suggestion the governors waived one fee, and Georgette and I embarked on a school life at St Michael's which we both remember with great affection.

St Michael's was a small school by today's standards — only about 300 of us in a pleasant building set in lovely grounds. Every memory I have is a good one. I loved above all the warmth of the nun and lay teachers and the sense of community amongst us all. Learning was without pressure. Standards at the school were always high and I realise now that it was due to the happiness of the place. We had a healthy ongoing rivalry between the four school 'houses'. I was in the 'Greens' (St Agnes House) and was so proud of every team achievement. In my day, we Greens were rather good at sport. This suited me fine. I was a member of the netball, tennis and gymnastic teams for both school and house. Greens and Golds kept winning school sports' trophies. Reds and Blues seemed the more academic.

Saturdays became taken up with sport. I usually played in a school match in the morning, rushed home to a lunch ready for me on the table, and then set off with Dad to football. I eventually became the Games

Captain of our house and then Head Girl of the school. I had obviously become, heart and soul, part of St Michael's spirit. I suspect now that it had a great deal to do with two teachers in particular.

Sister Teresa was my geography teacher and later she taught me religious studies when I was in her form. She had a great influence on me. We all loved geography, captivated by her unfailing enthusiasm and hard work. We knew from the amount of effort that she put into her lessons that we were important to her. So important, in fact, that anything we were interested in she shared with us. Every Saturday morning she would be on the sideline cheering us on as we took on the local schools at netball or tennis. I always shared with her a friendly rivalry because she was house-mistress of the Gold Team.

My own house-mistress was the classics teacher, Sister John Vianney. I was pretty awful at Latin and so I never had the benefit of her classes. I was sorry about this because I recognised that she was one of the kindest teachers we had. I admired her from a distance.

Looking back I am quite sure that it was the influence of these two sisters that put the idea of religious life into my head. I am convinced that it is people who influence us, not abstract ideals or well thought-out arguments. I was so happy at St Michael's that it seemed a very good idea to discover more about the life of the community.

One dinner hour I was summoned to the headmistress, Sister Clare Dominic. I arrived breathless in my PE kit, fresh from team practice, and was startled when she asked me, 'What are you going to do when you leave school?' I took a deep breath and said, 'Be a nun, I think'. It was the first time I had admitted it to anyone, but having articulated it I immediately felt confident that I would indeed enter the convent. I was thirteen years old. From that day on I never doubted the wisdom of my choice and I never thought of doing anything else. I certainly didn't tell my friends for a long time. Perhaps they guessed. Sister Teresa surely did when I asked her to lend me the life story of the foundress of the order.

I liked what I read. Clare Fey was the daughter of a factory owner in Aachen, Germany. Unlike so many earlier industrialists, Herr Fey refused to take on child labour. Clare grew up with his example before her. She began 'poor schools' for the street children and in turn, her example spread to her friends. From these beginnings a new religious congregation was formed. The sisters quietly challenged the injustices meted out to poor families by the new industrial rich. They fed and educated neglected children so that they no longer had to slave in the factories to survive.

The congregation grew swiftly. In 1872, only twenty-eight years after the formal foundation of the congregation, there were nearly seven hundred sisters working in twenty-five convents. But in that year a religious persecution swept through Germany and twenty-two of the convents were immediately closed. Clare Fey set about the task of finding new work and new homes for five hundred sisters abroad. A dozen German nuns arrived in England and settled in Southam, in Warwickshire. By the turn of the century the English branch of the Congregation was flourishing and a new foundation was made in Finchley.

By the time I entered the sixth form I was quite clear about my future. I wanted to enter with the sisters as soon as I finished school. On a school trip to Holland I had visited the motherhouse of the sisters and was impressed by the international reach of the congregation. There was always a great sense of joy amongst the sisters that I met, and I was really quite impatient to join them. But I still had a long wait ahead.

By now I had plucked up the courage to tell my parents of my decision. As I expected, my mother had no real objections except that she was concerned about the reaction of my father. It had always been Mum's wise practice to put no pressure on Dad to fall in with her religious convictions. I have heard of other Catholics who put intolerable pressure on their non-Catholic partners. In her usual perceptive way Mum always recognised Dad's right to his own beliefs. (The Catholic Church caught up with her later!) But this time was I asking too much? What on earth could Dad make of my crazy plans?

He was deeply upset. I was, after all, the one who shared hours of watching sport with him. We'd been to Lords for cricket and the White City for athletics, weekly football and annual amateur cup finals at Wembley. It seemed to him inconceivable that I could survive the solemn enclosed life of a nun. To play for time I agreed to go first to college and train for teaching. I dare say he hoped I'd grow out of the idea. I knew I wouldn't.

It was next stop Hull. I followed Georgette once again, this time to a Catholic training college. I launched straight into two happy years of college life. In between the tough schedule of lectures all day, 9.00 am to 8.00 pm plus Saturday mornings, I was able to get in a few visits to the Poor Child Jesus children's homes in Leeds and Sheffield. I was more than ever sure that my teacher training was just passing time until I could work with the children 'in care'. I opted for the Special PE course. Why not have a last fling at sport?

I really enjoyed college and to my surprise found myself on the student council and a student union representative. I even managed a distinction at the end of the course. I hadn't really expected to find teaching so enjoyable. There was no difficulty in getting jobs in those days and I took up my first teaching post in a large secondary modern school in Tottenham, not very far from the Spurs football ground at White Hart Lane.

It wasn't easy telling Dad, before the year was out, that I was giving in my notice and preparing to join the sisters. He was hurt and very silent about it. My headmaster was furious, saying I should have made known my intentions at the interview for the job. It all made me feel a bit heroic that I was making such an unpopular move.

It isn't very easy to look back and analyse the reasons for making decisions. But today's visit to Santa Clara has revived my great empathy with the spirit of Clare Fey's congregation. Clare found the presence of God in people and her work amongst children of the poor was always characterised by joy. In temperament I feel at home in this atmosphere. My theological ideas have changed over the years but I have never found a better way of expressing my deepest belief about God than that of Clare Fey: that he is not distant but present with us in people.

In September 1959 I left home for Southam, near Leamington Spa, to enter the novitiate. I knew it was a devastating blow to Dad and therefore difficult for Mum too. But strangely, when it came to it, my real sadness was leaving my brother. Georgette seemed to understand and she accompanied me to the convent that day, but Richard was only fourteen and I knew I was going to miss the important years of his growing up. At least he could take my place at football matches. And he did.

My first evening gave me a taste of the novitiate days ahead. I didn't even know if my father would visit me in

Southam. He had said that he could never do that. When I unpacked my case I showed the superior a box of soaps given to me by one of the pupils I had just left. I was quite taken aback when she took it from me and said, 'You don't need that. We have blocks of hard soap.' I felt I had arrived.

I changed my summer clothes for the black dress and short veil of a postulant, and began the novitiate stage of training in religious life. For the first six weeks postulants have no visitors, write no letters and have little to do even with the community. It is a quiet time of readjustment. I don't think I was at all surprised when, six weeks to the day, my family arrived. In spite of everything, Dad was there to give support. With that reassurance I was ready to launch wholeheartedly into the new adventure.

3 NOVICE

DIARY August 3

Today we started to film with the BBC. But the day started badly, with Pedro feeling sick (yesterday's lunch? altitude sickness? nerves?). He took only a sip of water for breakfast. He brightened up during the day, and finished keeping the whole BBC crew amused by playing on the name of the Norfolk assistant cameraman, Roy (Toy Boy, Joy Boy, Coy Boy — and eventually in the Norfolk accent Moy Boy, Croy Boy etc.).

We went first to Andrès Fey School. Our purpose was to meet up again with one of the teachers, Sister Martha Lucia. Nine years ago she had spent her university vacation bringing Pedro and Blanca back to life. The BBC arrived early, to set the scene, so that what they filmed was live, not artificially re-enacted. (Poor Pedro was sick as we arrived at the door.) In fact the meeting was joyful, spontaneous and highly emotional. We couldn't have acted it over again.

Sister hasn't changed. She is the same warm, sensitive, joyous person we met nine years ago. To our sorrow we found that, although only in her early thirties, she needs a hip-replacement operation. She needs it urgently as she is in great pain and some days barely able to walk.

The inevitable convent parlour, drinks, and cakes. Pedro put a brave face on it all but was sick again. The community greeted us and asked us why we weren't staying with them over these days. What a relief. We said we'd move in at once! Pedro recovered.

We were escorted into the happy school, built in one of the poorest suburbs of the city. Smiling pupils greeted us at every turn and shyly tried out their English. Pedro and Blanca are getting good at 'Muy bien, gracias' and 'Hasta la vista'. Whilst the BBC interviewed Martha Lucia, I found the spot in the garden, under the tree, where on our previous visit Mother Teresina, the Superior, had told me about my letter of 1960. It is good to be here.

When I was a novice in Southam in 1960 we heard that our congregation was going to set up an international novitiate for training missionaries. It would be based in the 'motherhouse', in Simpelveld on the Dutch-German border.

I was immediately interested. It seemed to me that the poverty of the Third World was similar to the poverty of nineteenth-century newly industrialised towns of Europe. In my enthusiastic way I wanted to live as closely as I could to the lifestyle of Clare Fey and her friends. So I wrote to the Superior General, Mother Beata Maria, and asked if I could transfer to Simpelveld, to train for Colombia. I eventually received a negative reply.

I had almost forgotten that letter until nine years ago, when the Colombian Superior, Mother Teresina, took me to Andrès Fey School. We sat under the tree in the garden and she told me a surprising story. 'Twenty years ago, in 1960,' she said, 'Mother Beata Maria visited us from Simpelveld. She was looking for a piece of land in a poor suburb to build a new convent where she hoped to end her days when she was no longer superior general. We bought this land. One morning we sat under this tree and she produced a letter from an English novice who wanted to come out to Bogota. That was you, wasn't it?' I was amazed to be reminded of that far-off request! And I was overjoyed when the kindly Mother Teresina continued that she could now rejoice at the decision they made to refuse my transfer to Colombia. 'The time is right for you to be here now, isn't it?'

So here I was again in Andrès Fey, the convent especially dear to Mother Beata Maria, a nun of the stature of Mother Teresa of Calcutta. She was one of those rare people whose presence was a grace. She had that silent authority of people whose lives are all goodness. Not a sentimental sweet goodness but a goodness that is strong in its total, uncompromising option for the poor. I had only met her twice face to face, but it was enough to convince me that I had met a truly 'holy' person. I therefore never questioned for one moment the letter of refusal.

I put my mind to my novitiate training in England. I took the name of Sister Clare. Nuns train for about six years before a final commitment. After six months' introduction, known as postulancy, there are two years as a novice, followed by temporary vows for three years. There were never many of us in the novitiate in my day. I was the only novice in my year so it was quite lonely at times. This was especially so in the first year because it was spent entirely in the novitiate itself, removed from the school and the children's home, and even from the Southam community. This was the year of training in spiritual direction, theology of religious life and scripture. It was a hot-house of religion. Strangely we never discussed anything; it was all talks given by the novice mistress. We were not expected to ask any questions. I've heard some former nuns speak of the harsh way they were treated by their superiors and novice mistress, as a way of testing their humility and obedience. I suppose religious orders founded in the nineteenth century inherited Victorian values. Children should be seen and not heard. Authority figures had to be obeyed without question. We were certainly treated like children. But my novice mistress was not hard. She commanded my deep respect.

At times I was confused by the ideas we were expected to accept without question. One day I was told that it was my turn to lead the community office chant. Since I have no singing voice, I was astounded that it could be exposed to the community in public, in church. I think Sr Stephen, my novice mistress, was just as embarrassed as I was. Years later she confided to me that she knew our training in religious life was all wrong. I expect she made all the same mental reservations that I made. When we had read to us at table the lives of the saints I remember thinking how foolish some recommendations were. We were expected to admire the obedience of a monk who spent hours planting cabbages upside down in the garden. I'm afraid I thought it was an insult to human intelligence. But I had learnt to keep my objections silent long before I entered the convent. When I was about eleven years old one elderly nun asked me if I was praying every day for my father. 'Why?' I asked. 'Because unless he becomes a Catholic he will not go to heaven.' I looked at the old lady and thought to myself, 'How stupid! You can't know my dad, and I don't think you know God either.'

But I didn't question most of the instruction about religious life we were given. And I certainly should have done. We were encouraged to think of ourselves as highly privileged human beings, chosen by God for a higher form of life than all others. We had a vocation that set us apart from the worldly. Our celibate state was superior to marriage. That kind of theology has, thank God, been repudiated by most of today's theologians. But years of treating nuns (and priests) as mortals set apart on pedestals has left its indelible mark.

Scratch many a lay Catholic and they will presume that they are not really as Christian as the nuns and priests. I believe that this has done terrible damage to the Church by distorting the gospel.

In my second year of novitiate I was introduced to the active work of the community. Hardly surprising that my first task was teaching. The first day back in the classroom was a nightmare. I had trained for secondary education but an infant teacher had fallen sick and I was called in to take over her class. I had no idea what to do with thirty five-year-olds all day. By the end of the third day I was near to despair. Children sense when the adults are not in control! It was convent 'theology' that obedience made every thing right. I think I felt guilty that I really couldn't manage without any expertise in the understanding and the teaching of the very young. Fortunately the sick teacher recovered. I retreated gratefully to the novitiate.

Second year novices have what today we would call 'work experience'. We would be sent around the convent to work in the laundry, the kitchen or the sacristy. And we had our turn on the rota to supervise meals, bedtime or 'recreation' time with the boarders. The Southam complex included a primary school and a children's home. I had looked forward to working at last with the children in care. The reality was not much easier than the foray into the infant class.

There were two houses of children, each of about a dozen youngsters. Many of them had had very unhappy early years and their insecurity and resentment of adults was understandable. Looking back I am amazed at how patient they were putting up with a rota of nuns doing their turn at supervision. I am ashamed now that I harboured very critical thoughts of the nun in charge of one house. She seemed to resent the help we were giving, saying she would stay with the children and we could go and help out with their laundry or meals. Of course she was trying to give them some security and build a closer relationship with them. The pity was we never discussed this and we were never given any training in child-care, even in basic psychology. I shudder at the damage we probably did to some children.

For a short while I slept in a dormitory with six young boys. One little lad, Francis, was staying with us because his mother was dying of cancer. I woke early one morning to the sound of his sobbing. Just imagine, I hesitated to go to him because it meant breaking the Great Silence, which forbade us to speak between 9.00 pm and about 8.00 am. I actually did go to him, but was restrained from holding the distressed little six-year-old boy because of my novice scruples. My instinct was to hug him and sit with him until he went back to sleep. I didn't do that. I just whispered soothing words and returned to bed. With the morning came the news that his mother had died in the night. I always regret that I wasn't sitting with him.

Hardly surprising that our naivety in dealing with very hurt children brought some worrying and awful moments. At one stage I got to dread my shift. We had a highly disturbed, hyperactive boy, Robert, who was a danger to others and to himself. I remember days when he would climb on to the roof of the tall school building and hurl slates down at the children in the playground. I had no idea how to deal with him. It can only have done him severe harm because each nun on the supervision rota probably dealt with him in a different way. How could he know where he stood? I became very confused about the role of a religious community caring for disturbed and damaged children. When I once heard an elderly nun threatening a difficult little girl (she was a sexually abused child) with God's punishment of her I was horrified. Thankfully most of the nuns in my community would never have spoken like that.

Nowadays when people get to know that I was in a convent I am likely to be regaled with their convent memories. I get two different responses. First there is the positive response. Those who recall with affection dear old Sister Ethelfridis who fussed and amused them; or the prim and polished discipline of the nun teachers who instilled in them ladylike qualities. They are proud of it now, though it was irksome at the time. Many of these speak with nostalgia of their school days and some still keep contact with the sisters.

But there is also a negative response. I have been told, 'The nuns were cruel. I hated it at school because we were humiliated and made to feel so guilty.' These people are probably the victims of a religious arrogance which used to plague our convents. It was often assumed that nuns did not need professional training for their job. It was enough that you were chosen by God for work in the order, and the spiritual life was supposed to make you fit to work with people. You were not supposed to get too close to people anyway because this would interfere with your relationship with God. Consequently some totally unsuitable individual nuns will have inflicted misery on their charges. The story is told of the teacher-nun who slapped the head of a distracted little girl, and shouted at her: 'You weren't listening. I said "God LOVES little children."' It is a funny story, but too many people have memories of nuns, priests or brothers who seemed to have sadistic streaks in their personality.

After the novitiate I made temporary profession of vows and received the black veil. To my surprise I was sent back to St Michael's in Finchley to teach part-time, alongside Sister Teresa and Sister John Vianney. My family were delighted to have me 'just round the corner'. I continued my religious studies by attending theology and scripture courses in London, with nuns of other congregations. It was a very happy time. I had the easy task of taking first-formers for general subjects. They were well-behaved, friendly middle-class girls. We never had discipline problems. The only time I remember a class questioning my authority was when I was pontificating to fifteen-year-olds about marriage. Young Brigid politely asked: 'Sister Clare, what do YOU know about it?' I had the audacity of my youthful enthusiasm to attempt to persuade her that I did know all the answers.

I was accepted for final profession and spent the immediate preparation for this in Rome and Simpelveld, in the motherhouse of the congregation. I was delighted that I was celebrating this important step at the heart of things, in the church where Clare Fey was buried and surrounded by an international group of sisters. My family even travelled over to Holland to celebrate the day with me.

The journey to Rome was not without incident. When I arrived at Dover I joined a long queue for the boat-train. In front of me was a harassed mum with a toddler and an older disgruntled child. Their dad had gone off to find a sandwich and was too long gone. Behind me another mother did not have enough arms to restrain a wandering toddler, hold the baby and guard her luggage. To my utter embarrassment a sailor came along the line of waiting families and invited me to follow him. 'The captain invites you on board first, Sister.' I walked ahead of everyone, was greeted by the captain and given a seat in a first-class position. I can only suspect that he was a Catholic captain who felt he must pay respect to a nun. It made me feel very uncomfortable. I really didn't want to be treated as a privileged person. It was a direct contrast to the gospel Jesus, whose life I wanted to follow. It worried me all the way to Rome, an awful journey as we had to make unscheduled stops, change trains and finally arrive, hours late, in the wrong station. I buried the whole disquiet as a last minute 'temptation' to my vocation!

I returned to England as a full member of the congregation, and took up a new teaching job back in Southam. I was relieved that I had the eleven-year-olds this time, not the infants. It was typical of convent practice that I was appointed deputy head — with little experience of course and in preference to older lay staff. The few years I spent there were hard going. My starry-eyed view of religious life was severely tested. I had expected a warmth in community life and the reality turned out to be something different. I seemed to have little in common with my headmistress and the elderly sisters were torn between showing their natural affection and the rigidity of their upbringing. It was specifically stated in the Rule Book that nuns must have no 'particular friends'. We were supposed to find all our joy in the friendship of God, in prayer. I don't think I ever really understood this. My instinct said that I needed people to love. When I meditated on the words of St John 'Whoever does not love does not know God, for God is love', I came to the conclusion that we needed to come closer to one another as real people. At times I remember feeling very depressed and I could never put my finger on the cause.

When my provincial superior told me that I was to return to London for an interview to attend a catechetical college, Corpus Christi, I was relieved. I was accepted as a student by the principal, Father Hubert Richards.

4 DOUBTS

DIARY August 4

More filming today, this time in the poorer parts of Bogota. First to the oldest part of town, the Belen district. The sight of children and adults picking at the rubbish thrown out of the market was shocking. Pedro and Blanca were rather silent, stunned by the utter poverty. The reality is so much worse than the pictures we see on television or in magazines. We all felt bad about filming here, voyeurs as it were into people's misery.

Drove in the BBC minibus to the convent the Sisters have established in this part of town. Here was a happier scene. Every day over 400 children arrive at the door to be fed, washed, baby-sat or educated. The sister explained to us that here, in this deprived city slum, many are one-parent children, some cared for only by their fathers. Death in childbirth is common. We were all captivated by the baby rooms: rows and rows of cots with sleeping, wriggling, smiling infants, and lines of little ones sitting on potties. The older children were in class. The sisters have built a medical and dental clinic for these families. Local doctors give their service free.

We left the convent with deep admiration for this community. They are selfless in standing alongside the poor, helping them to cope against all the odds. We sat on the church steps out in the street not ready to move on. The pull on the emotions is quite a thing. I caught the eye of one of the film crew, 'Clipboard Linda', and we didn't need to talk!

Next stop was a *favela*, a shanty town settlement on the

steep hills which border the city. This was a different type of poverty. The little lean-to huts sat untidily upon each other. Thin, scraggy dogs sniffed the dust and children with too old faces carried bundles up the steep slopes. But everyone smiled and greeted us with interest. Dick Meadows, our producer, set us up for an interesting shot. We had to walk twenty yards across a narrow swinging rope bridge which traversed a twenty-foot deep gully. Bert nearly fell off laughing when Pedro announced, 'I never thought the BBC was going to ask me to do death-defying stunts.'

Back to Andrès Fey to share with Martha Lucia our ambiguous thoughts about the poverty of South American cities. In cosy armchair–theology mood back in England it is so easy to offer solutions. We always applaud the financial help offered by the CAFODS, Christian Aids, Misereors and Trocairs of Europe. The sisters of the Poor Child Jesus can only build their schools and clinics with European aid. But a Colombian Jesuit, a university professor who opted to live in a shanty town hut, told us that he doesn't welcome outside help for his people. 'What happens', he said, 'if aid is stopped for any reason?' He was making the shanty-town dwellers aware of their own abilities to demand justice. They still lived in poverty but not destitution. They cared for each other and worked, with a sense of community, for gradual change. I suspect we capitalist westerners (Pope included) need to do much more listening and learning from the Third World.

I first got really aware of the struggle for justice in Third World countries when I moved to London in 1970. I moved out of my community into an international group of mature students at Corpus Christi College. It was a superb year of awakening to new ideas. After the rather closed confines of the community in rural Southam I found the energetic lay/religious, male/female, national/international community a breath of invigorating air. Our college was situated near a house for destitute women run by Mother Teresa's Missionaries of Charity. I was able to spend time helping there — sometimes joining in the night soup-runs into the City.

My provincial superior was a woman of great intelligence and common sense. I think she would have loved to go to the college herself. Instead she sent me and insisted that I live in at the college, 'or else you won't feel that you are really part of it'.

Emotionally, spiritually and theologically I grew up during that year. All my studying in the convent had been directed at finding sure answers. Traditional Catholic theology 'knows' the answer to everyone's questioning. I learnt at Corpus Christi that I didn't even know the right questions to ask. And I learnt that we are all searching for answers, especially in our religious lives. I look back now and am surprised that the discovery did not rock my faith. Quite the reverse. I was, (and still remain) excited by the uncertainty of faith. I am sure that my confidence was due to the brilliant teaching of the staff. The willingness to listen to other people and to question ultimate values makes for a healthy community life. They encouraged this and they stood alongside us and never intruded with ready-made answers. I learnt more about the Christian life from the atmosphere of the college than from any wordy lectures. St Francis is supposed to have said to his companions, 'Go out and preach the gospel. If necessary use words.' My Corpus Christi year made good sense of that.

There was considerable tension in the English Province of my Congregation at the time I went to the college. There had been unrest since the Church itself had begun asking questions. Pope John XXIII had set in motion a quiet revolution when he called a meeting of the Catholic bishops, later known as the Second Vatican Council. This wise and kindly pope had decided it was time for the Catholic Church to take stock and enter the twentieth century. Every aspect of theology, spirituality and practice came under the spotlight for examination. After years of discussion the Council issued, from 1963 to 1965, sixteen major statements in a series of long documents.

Many of the decisions made at the Council, especially those referring to the life of nuns, created an immediate tension and anxiety in communities around the world. Change is never easy. The religious congregations engaged in social activities were called upon to rewrite their rules and constitutions. It was a case of adapting the ancient monastic life to a more realistic lifestyle for those engaged in teaching, nursing or child-care. Many nuns and priests at this time began to question their role in the Church. And many felt threatened by the movement of renewal.

I had made my final profession in 1965, just as the Vatican Council concluded its work. A challenging way to start life as a full member of the Congregation. But not too comfortable. Inevitably views polarised, for or against change. Perhaps surprisingly, it was some of my superiors who urged us to go ahead with renewal quickly. It was a struggle for them because of deep resistance from many sisters. I don't think that active religious life in the 'First World' has ever found its role since those days.

To complicate matters for our Congregation the whole secular child-care movement in Europe was in a state of change. Children's homes were closing down in favour of family care. Adoption and fostering were encouraged to avoid the damaging effects of institutionalised care. So we needed to look for different ways of helping the young. Five of us started a new venture in Holloway, North London. We moved from the larger Finchley community into a small house in a residential area near the women's prison. When the Catholic prison chaplain asked for help in his work I jumped at the idea.

For two years I worked alongside Father David Evans in the prison. He could only talk to the women in his office, but I could spend informal time with them, in their cells or on their corridors. I was in the happy position of having no professional role. This meant that many women could relax and share their worries, because 'you, Sister, aren't going to write me up in a report.' I loved being there, and was somewhat shaken to find that the sense of community amongst the women often put my religious community experience to shame. The suffering of many of the prisoners made them generous and sensitive to their companions. They certainly showed for each other greater compassion than I witnessed from some of the officers, who could be quite brutal.

I was bitterly disappointed when, at one of our countless community meetings, my work in the prison was questioned: 'It isn't being true to the spirit of Mother Clare who worked with children', was the complaint. I hadn't thought like that at all. I was intent on holding to her spirit of compassion for damaged, hurt people. And there they were on our doorstep. The Superior General came from Simpelveld to give her verdict. I took her round the prison and she was shocked to see girls as young as fourteen on the remand wing. When one young woman asked me for a rosary (what good timing!) she gave away hers and gave me permission to continue visiting. She told the sisters that it was an unusual work for our Congregation, but I could be made an exception. I should have been delighted but it cast a shadow of discomfort. I didn't want to be an exception — that way I was on the edge of the Congregation. I wanted to be at its heart.

My prison work was part-time. I needed to earn a wage too. I did this by helping out at the Catholic Information Office, where we produced documentation of church decisions and renewal programmes. Since the Vatican Council numerous working commissions had been set up and their reports stacked our offices. I enjoyed the variety of situations the work presented to me, especially when it involved meeting with people working for renewal. At one time I was invited to the British Council of Churches as they prepared for a forthcoming Assembly of the World Council of Churches in Java, Indonesia. No sooner had I mentioned that my Congregation had convents in Java, than I was invited to go along with the delegates to work behind the scenes in Jakarta. I was thrilled and enthusiastically presumed there would be no problem. My fare was going to be paid.

My request was put to the Provincial Chapter of the Congregation which was meeting at that time. This governing group was made up of the superiors and elected delegates from each convent in the English Province. I happened to be a delegate myself, so I looked forward to sharing my exciting news with everyone. I was totally unprepared for the reaction of some of the sisters. Murmurs of interest and approval were silenced by the strong protest of two of them. A Southam sister was adamant that it was quite wrong to attach oneself to the World Council of Churches. 'The Catholic Church does *not* work with this organisation, which gives money to terrorist groups. Your presence there would bring trouble on the Congregation.' That view made me very sad, but it was the intervention of a superior which devastated me. 'I am most unhappy', she said, 'at Sister Clare's enthusiasm. When will she learn to settle down and be content with a humdrum life in the convent like everyone else?' I was speechless. My former novice mistress was angry and spoke up for me. And I could see that the other superiors were sympathetic. But I left the meeting in tears, not because I couldn't go to Java, but because my very character had been called into question. I knew that it was my enthusiasm for life which had brought me into the convent. If it was wrong for me to enter wholeheartedly into things as a nun then I wasn't in the right place. I believe, even now, that the sister was quite wrong and that I had the support of most of the community. But somehow I was never completely happy again. I found that I was being my extrovert, eager self with outsiders to the community. I hesitated to share anything with my sisters in case it was misunderstood.

A few weeks later the venue of the Assembly of the World Council of Churches was changed to Nairobi because of protests by the Muslim majority in Indonesia.

It is probably true to say that I spent the next two years looking for reasons to stay in the convent. One novice after another left us, and even professed sisters began to leave too. Many outsiders suspect that nuns and priests usually leave their convents or presbyteries because of problems with celibacy. This will be true of some, but it certainly had nothing to do with my own eventual decision to leave. Of the three vows I had professed, 'poverty, chastity and obedience', chastity was the least difficult to observe. I honestly cannot remember having sexual difficulties. Having made the decision to forego an intimate relationship and family life I didn't dwell on what I was 'missing'.

In retrospect I can see that my understanding of the vow of chastity (as I was taught in novitiate days) was putting a great strain on my relationships, both inside and outside of the community. By nature I am a real extrovert. My instinct is to respond to people with warmth and closeness. I was always afraid of getting too close to others because my vow was to set me apart for God. We were warned about 'particular friendships' — loving people was a danger. But I was never consciously troubled by unfulfilled sexual needs.

I spent many years trying to understand my vow of poverty. I never succeeded. I believe to this day that it is a very strange and ambiguous promise made by religious. I was never materially poor as a nun. Life in a community is, by its very definition, protected from the uncertainty and discomfort of poverty as experienced by millions in the world. Nuns are well fed, well housed, well protected, well travelled. Someone said to me recently, 'Why is it that there are always groups of nuns at airports?' We were told that poverty was not to do with possessions and having a roof over our head, but with detachment from these things. We could have tape recorders, typewriters — anything we needed, but we mustn't be attached to them. It was the spirit of poverty that mattered: 'Blessed are the poor in spirit.' I remember once having a cold and being persuaded by the convent infirmarian to stay in bed for a day or two. 'They can get on without you in school. Go to bed and I'll bring you a hot drink.' Tucked up and cossetted I recalled, with a sense of unease, an occasion when I was about seven years old. Our whole family was staying with relations in order to share a Christmas pantomime visit. My mother spent the whole of Peter Pan sniffing

into her handkerchief. She had a shocking cold. My
Dad and Aunt encouraged her to sleep longer the next
morning — a Sunday. Making no fuss Mum just quietly
replied that if she could go to the pantomime she was
well enough to go to Mass. I never forgot it. I thought in
my seven-year-old way that there must be something
very special about going to church. Mum, like all
mothers, never went to bed when she was feeling ill.
That's poverty.

It seemed to me that we kidded ourselves very well
that we were living a life of poverty. When we were sick
we were cared for; we had our meals cooked for us, our
laundry washed for us. We had no need to worry about
paying rent or getting jobs, and our future old age was
protected. Once when I was working in the prison a nun
from another congregation asked the Governor if she
could spend the night in a prison cell. 'I want to feel
what it is like to be in prison,' she said, 'so that I can
share the women's poverty.' I thought to myself, 'What
a silly woman. She has chosen to stay locked up. She
will get out next morning. She has a community who
cares about her. She will be praised for spending a night
behind bars. She is as far away as ever from their bitter
experience.'

So I was always uneasy about religious poverty. I
sensed that it was leading us all into an unreal world. I
only interpreted my misgivings years later when I had
left the convent. One Sunday at Mass the gospel reading exhorted us not to worry about tomorrow because
God will provide, just as he provides for the lilies of the
field and the birds of the air. In his sermon the young
priest told us that this passage was not for us, but only
for the priests and nuns who had taken a vow of poverty. 'They have no need to be concerned for material
things,' he said; 'God will provide for them through

you, the laity. You have to be concerned about worldly goods. God provides for those who have chosen him.' I was speechless at this travesty of the Christian gospel. Every Christian is called to respond to the gospel. The priest was making his vow a vow of privilege, not a vow of poverty. Of course, every priest doesn't speak like that, but it explained to me how confusing the vow can be.

The third vow I promised for life was that of obedience. This was a straightforward option when I entered the convent in 1959. I expected to be told what to do in every detail of my life. I knew it would be difficult but with youthful enthusiasm that didn't worry me. My superiors would be the mouthpiece for God. They would interpret his will for me. I soon learnt that this was a fine way to transfer all responsibility for my life over to others.

I started off with eagerness. Nothing too dramatic was asked of me. The first time it was difficult to obey was during my second year noviciate. The two first-year novices and myself were left some gospel study to complete whilst our novice mistress was away. I produced pages of commentary and presented it illustrated with poetry and art pictures. I was expecting to be praised for my hard work, but Sr Stephen pointed out that it was thoughtless to present it so well when the younger novices who were less academic than myself could not match it. The rebuff didn't do me any harm except confuse me. Later with the Vatican Council recommendations we younger sisters were encouraged to do our best at everything. (And Sr Stephen was the first to recognise the about-turn.) More confusing still, we were consulted about our future work. God's will was now seen in our own aptitudes and preferences.

I don't blame my Congregation for any of the

confusion. The sisters were all struggling to find the way forward as communities of witness to the gospel. There was no ill will. In times of change it is hard for everyone. European Christianity is very tired. There is constant self-examination. Our visit to the Belen community has brought home to me one fundamental reason why active religious life is currently on the decline in Europe. It is our Western materialism and capitalist ideology. Materialism has blurred our vision and blunted the edge of our convictions. There are very few Christians today who offer a clear challenge to the selfish way we live in the West. There are few Christians willing to rock the boat of our complacent society. Religious life has to rise out of the Christian community of its time. A sleepy Christianity isn't likely to produce dynamic religious communities. Religious life itself has become affected by these corrosive capitalist values.

But in the Third World things are different. When a hungry child or a sick man sits on your doorstep the idea of religious poverty as a 'spiritual detachment from possessions' sounds very thin. The Sisters have to understand and practise their vow of poverty in relation to their people's destitution.

In the misery of down-town slum Bogota my Sisters have only one common purpose, to bring relief to the suffering people. That aim brings a richer community life with little time or energy for continual self-examination. Community life is strengthened by the needs of the neighbourhood. Little wonder that religious life flourishes in the Third World and is on the decline in the First World.

5 LEAVING

DIARY August 5

I got up early this morning to join the sisters and
school children at a 7.00 am Mass in the school hall.
The quietness and concentration of the girls was
impressive. Two teachers and a girl played guitars.
Pupils did the readings and led the prayers —
including one for Pedro and Blanca. The priest cast
the only sombre note. As a school chaplain he was not
good news. He took himself far too seriously, no
smiles, no light touches and no eye-to-eye contact. I
noticed later that he sat alone for breakfast fussed
over by one of the community. Priests here are still
the ones 'set apart'. I can just see Jesus having his
Galilee fish breakfast in one room and his disciples
sitting together next door!

Spent much of the day with Sister Martha Lucia. The
children were relieved to have time to themselves to play
in their room. Pedro has taken to lying on his bed
reading. Giggles tell us that he is enjoying Rouald Dahl.
Bert got down to his diary and disappeared into the
garden to do a sketch. I had the luxury of an hour or two
in the laundry, discovering how therapeutic it is to wash
by hand on marble slabs.

Later we all went shopping with Martha Lucia. Being
with her is happiness. She has made a deep impression on
the BBC team who recognise that she is someone special.
We sat up very late tonight with her playing board games
in Spanish and English. Remarkable how quickly the
children have learnt some Spanish. They are also very
smart at writing 'cinquaines', a little poetic form of

2,4,6,8,2 syllables (taught them by their excellent teacher at home). Today's efforts:

Shopping:
Looked ev'rywhere.
Found a good place at last.
Mummy and Blanca went quite mad:
No cash!

Drawing:
It is great fun.
I drew Dad with his pipe.
When he saw it he burst his sides.
Peasant!

The latter was put together by Pedro with a little help from his dad. It's a lovely sight when Pedro and Bert sit together with sketch pads and laugh over the results. Perhaps the nicest part of this journey is going to be the hours we spend together with little to do but laugh, relax and share our interests. We are so blessed that the children need very little to make them content.

This day spent with Sr Martha Lucia at Andrès Fey Convent would hardly rate in travel brochures as a highlight experience of a holiday. But for me it has been a special day in the trip. I am very content here surrounded by a community in which I feel so much at home. Martha Lucia and I had a long talk about my decision to leave the Congregation. We understand each other very well. She is a strong-minded, warm-hearted woman who is not afraid to be critical in a constructive way. I would have liked to be with her in community.

In 1974, three years after I had completed my year in Corpus Christi College, I wrote again to the Superior General (a recently elected German sister) and asked a second time if I could go and join the sisters in South America. The reply was again in the negative. It was my last attempt to stay in the convent. A few months later I made the most difficult decision of my life — to ask for a dispensation from my vows. If I had been allowed to join a community like Andrès Fey, I sometimes wonder whether I would still be in the Congregation. In all honesty I think it would only have delayed my decision.

The three years that followed the Corpus Christi experience were not easy ones. My exposure to a newer theology inevitably distanced me from most of the community. They, like many Catholics, were highly suspicious of new theological ideas. It didn't help the situation when my bishop, Cardinal Heenan of Westminster, entered into a great controversy with the college. During my year there we received an extraordinary visit from the entire Catholic hierarchy of bishops. They were assembled at the college over three days because the Cardinal was beginning to have cold feet about allowing Catholics to enter the theological/scripture debate of the time. I imagine he was bombarded with complaints from conservative quarters about the freedom with which these modern theologians and their students were questioning the old values — even the sacred 'doctrines'.

One morning during the New Year break I was at breakfast with the Finchley community. We listened to the 8 o'clock news over our bacon. To my amazement and dismay I heard the announcer say that Cardinal Heenan had issued a statement to the effect that he had accepted the resignation of the entire staff of Corpus Christi College. This was news to staff and students alike. The press statement caused havoc and led to a public debate about the conflict between the Cardinal and scholars. The staff, led by Father Hubert Richards, were respected and admired across the world. The college had sent out its mature students to take up responsible positions in catechetical circles in the five continents.

Those of us who were students at this time shared in a personal way the distress and pain of the staff. The Cardinal appointed a replacement staff for the following year's courses. The 'new' Corpus Christi never recovered the blow or had the inspiration of the first college and it closed down after two years.

The timing of this episode was critical for those of us attending the college. For weeks the press published the arguments that the Archbishop's decision had raised, and conservative Catholics in our communities were given fuel for their anxieties about the 'dangerous new doctrines'. Every weekend when I returned to Finchley I found newspaper cuttings in my pigeon-hole. They were heavily underlined and annotated with warnings! The Cardinal had spoken and acted, and he was infallible.

One of Cardinal Heenan's greatest concerns was that many former students of the college had opted to leave the religious life and the priesthood. He put this down to the relaxed, warm friendships that the atmosphere of the place encouraged. He was shocked that students and staff called each other by Christian names. One visitor was even horrified to see that the cubbyholes for our briefcases were in simple alphabetical order, with nuns indiscriminately mixed with priests and lay people. She had to be assured we did not sleep in the cubbyholes!

Heenan felt that the free and familiar mixing of priests with nuns was a danger to chastity. No doubt he acted with his own integrity, supported by the anxieties of many of the bishops. But the real issue was the emerging of a new understanding of God and of people which challenged the older, static concepts of traditional theology. It is best described in the language of a 'one-world' or 'two-world' theology.

The 'two-world' outlook is the view held by traditional Christians. God is a transcendent father who created our world and in his omnipotence can alter its rules if he so wills. Mankind has glimpses of this heavenly being especially in the person of Jesus who is, in fact, divine because he is God's own Son. People should live their lives with one eye on heaven for that is their true home. There are two worlds, the world of God and the world of mankind. Everything on earth is temporary, in fact this 'world' is a distraction. People should put most of their effort into a spiritual life because it is in prayer that they will reach God and know his will. True riches are in heaven, which means that the poor can be comforted that they will be rewarded when they die — if they have lived good lives. God sometimes alters the rules of the universe to help people or to punish the wicked.

The 'one-world' view approaches God from the opposite end. All that can be known of God is known through the human experience. God, the ground of all being, the reality behind all of creation, is best understood in terms of love. God is most clearly seen in the life of the human Jesus. The love and compassion he showed was unique. He was like a window into the nature of God — therefore he is called God's own son. Whoever shows such Godlike love is also making God really present in the world. God, the creator, who made people in 'his own image', is tied down by his creation. People have the freedom to use their gifts for good or evil and God cannot intervene by altering his laws to patch up mistakes. There is one world only, this world. People are all called to make it grow towards its perfection; poverty, injustice, greed and hatred prevent people from seeing God in his world, and distort God's plan. Prayer does not alter God's mind, it serves to alter our opinions and behaviour.

These two theologies are worlds apart. Literally! My description is an over-simplification of course. Christians may well hover between the two poles. When I arrived at the college I had never really analysed my understanding of God. He certainly belonged to a 'two-world' theology. A year later, in our final seminar, attended by all the students and staff, we had a look at the positions we then held. I told the group that I liked to think I was now a 'one-world' thinker, but that I suspected it was nearer to a 'one-and-a-quarter world'.

Without any doubt my newer thinking distanced me from many of the sisters. I remember a November feast of the Holy Souls as one such occasion. It was a tradition in the Catholic Church to pray on November 2 for those who had died. It was understood that the souls had gone to a resting place, en route for heaven. This was purgatory, a place of suffering, which was punishment for sin and a purifying in preparation for life in heaven. In the Middle Ages a custom had grown up that encouraged people to gain an indulgence, or remission of punishment, on behalf of the souls in purgatory. One way to gain these indulgences was to say six 'Our Fathers', six 'Hail Marys' and six 'Glory Bes' in church on November 2. It was one indulgence per visit. I was in the chapel after breakfast when one elderly nun whispered hurried prayers, got up, ran to the door then back to her bench, whispered more hurried prayers and repeated her toing and froing over and over again. She was still there at dinner time. She was trying to get in as many three-times-six prayers as she could, to get God to save souls from purgatory. Perhaps it did no harm to the old lady — at least she felt she was doing some good for others. But I found the whole exercise a ludicrous understanding of a loving God.

It was incidents like these that gnawed away at me until I decided that I probably couldn't spend the rest of my life in constant self-analysis and in a hot-house religious atmosphere. There was no blinding light when I suddenly 'knew' that I had to leave. It was exactly as Metropolitan Anthony, the Russian Orthodox bishop, had predicted when I shared with him my anxieties and questions about religious life. 'You'll wake up one day,' he said, 'and make a decision with no drama, no visions, just a certainty and a peace that you are going to follow wherever God leads without constant re-examination of motives. What that means in practice,' he explained, 'is that you will simply choose what will enable you to be most true to your own temperament and nature. You are not in the right place if you can't act always in the most loving way.'

He was quite right. I woke up one morning and knew that I was going to leave the Congregation. There was no specific incident that sparked off the final decision. I have no idea why that morning seemed different to others. I just felt a great sense of relief and peace.

I saw our new Provincial Superior, Sister Ursula, and she was generous and kind in her reaction. Perhaps she was expecting my request. It can't have been easy for her especially as her predecessor had herself decided to leave the Congregation not many months previously. Sister Ursula asked if I wanted more time to think about it, perhaps some quiet days of reflection? I knew that wasn't necessary. I was over weary of self-analysis.

I sometimes wonder now if the constant soul-searching which is part of religious life actually contributed to my departure. All nuns spend time in community prayer and in private prayer. There is a time for the daily meditation and for a daily examination of conscience. Many people seem to envy the nuns these hours of private prayer. I have to say that I never found meditation attractive. And the daily examination of self had begun to feel like a neurotic preoccupation with myself. It all seemed to be 'Me and God'. I found this increasingly irritating, a rather selfish luxury that we enjoyed. Even now, fifteen years on, I am embarrassed at the amount of time some sisters spend on spiritual renewals, thirty-day retreats, courses on spirituality. Is it a substitute for the fulfilment that lay people find in relating lovingly to others?

I don't deny that we all need times of quiet and reflection. We can't operate as balanced, happy people without an inner calm. But the insistence that we need to withdraw from people in order to meet God contradicts my understanding of the central Christian doctrine of the Incarnation. I take it to mean that God is present in the very heart of things — and that, for most people, means in the rush and muddle of everyday living. Too much insistence that we need to 'find time for God', or that we 'leave all our worries at the chapel door' gives me the very uncomfortable feeling that we are pushing our simple ordinariness into second place. This has, very effectively, made many lay Christians assume they are second-class Christians. The nuns and priests who have time for 'the spiritual life' are the real disciples of Jesus. This attitude is deeply ingrained in the Catholic community. An intelligent mother of five, a teacher, once remarked to me, 'Wouldn't it be wonderful to be a *real* Christian like the nuns, and have time to pray!'

I was very interested recently to read an article on Thomas Merton by Monica Furlong. She expressed exactly my own reservations about the ideal of religious solitude. She writes of Merton, the silent monk, 'He does *go on so* about solitude, about the business of being a hermit. What troubles me is the self-dramatising aspect of it. All this fuss about it, I caught myself thinking, and the world is full of men and women, voluntarily or involuntarily, living alone and making a go of it, without the kudos associated with "being a hermit". One of the dangers of living alone is of becoming entirely fascinated by and wrapped up in oneself.'

It didn't surprise me to hear that our Pastoral Centres for study and renewal are overbooked for spiritual retreats (especially those which concentrate on individual guidance) but are unable to attract people to weekend courses on justice, peace or reconciliation issues. The director of one of these Catholic centres asked, 'Why do people apparently value their relationship with God as of far greater importance than their relationship with their neighbours and the world God has made? Are not love for God and love for justice the same love?' A social worker, invited to talk on a weekend course for women, comments on the total contrast between the women dependent on social services and the Christian women who had the time, the leisure and the money to 'be able to afford a "spirituality" of this kind'. 'What', she asked, 'have the Churches to say to single mothers living in council flats on diminishing social security about spirituality?'

This was really the same question I was asking in 1974. 'Where do we find God? Is he in the middle of ordinary, unnoticed daily lives, or is he only attainable on a spiritual hotline?' I decided to opt for the former and take my chance on finding God in a more ordinary setting than the convent.

Sister Ursula explained the procedure for asking for a dispensation from religious vows and helped me in every way to prepare for leaving the Congregation. She

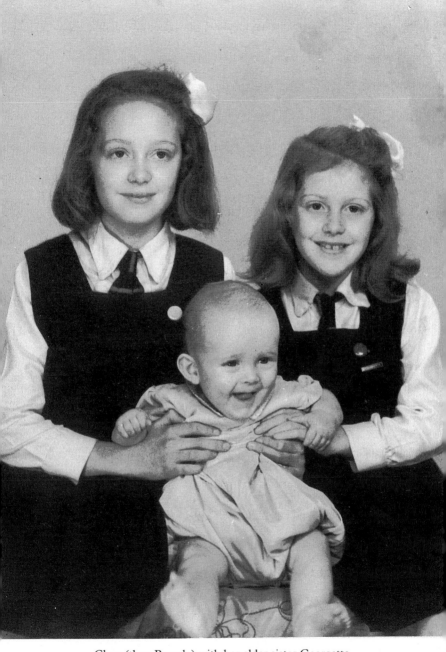

Clare (then Pamela) with her elder sister Georgette
and brother Richard

LEFT
Bert and Clare cut
their wedding cake

BELOW
Clare and Bert
arrive at Heathrow
carrying Pedro and Blanca

LEFT
Georgette holding
Blanca and Pedro

BELOW
Pedro and Blanca
at the age of five

Looking after the slum children of Belen

The Richards family with the nuns at Bosa
(Sr Martha Lucia second from right)

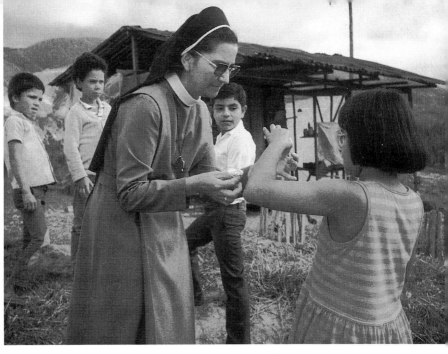

Blanca tries out her Spanish with Sr Claudia Angelica

Our first view of La Argentina

The children of La Argentina are fascinated by the BBC film crew

High Street, La Argentina

Blanca and Pedro embracing Maricela

The kitchen in Camilo's house

ABOVE
The Richards family
meet their
Colombian relatives

RIGHT
Delfina's grave

strongly advised that I should not actually leave the Holloway community until I had found a teaching job and accommodation. She gave me blank cheques to go and shop for clothes and everything I would need for my bedsit. Her kindness was remarkable.

I had to break the news to my family, community and friends. That wasn't easy. As I expected, my family were completely supportive and put no pressure on me to return home to them. I was grateful to be left free to have time to adjust on my own. I looked for a bedsit in London. At the same time I found a temporary teaching post in a school for maladjusted children in Harlesden. By this time my superiors had passed my request for dispensation from vows on to Rome, and received approval. Under Pope Paul VI there was no difficulty in obtaining the permission. Today it is more difficult. The present Pope, John Paul II, takes a different view on religious vows and is loth to release nuns from their commitment.

The worst part of all was leaving my small community in Holloway. I felt that I was letting them down. We had a very kind older sister who kept house for us. She did everything to make us comfortable. She was always there when we returned from our work and she had a fine meal ready on the table. I felt heartless because she loved to 'mother' us, and I was turning my back on her. I discovered that it was one thing 'leaving the Congregation' and quite another leaving the people I loved to be with. I don't think I slept a wink on my last night at the convent.

In the morning I packed my case, and took a last look at my cosy attic bedroom. I took off my gold ring and left it on the table beside my profession crucifix. It was a very sad moment.

6 MARRIAGE

DIARY August 6

Filming again today. The BBC van came at 8.30, and took us to the courtyard of a delightful colonial house in the old part of town, now an Arts and Crafts Centre. Weather unpromising with a little drizzle, so we shopped and sketched while we waited for it to clear. Eventually the cameraman got a good sequence of the children doing a slalom round the pillars of the courtyard — but it had to be taken six times, front, sideways, from the back, and from above — with several shots having to be scrapped because of noise intruding. Finally an interview with us, sitting by the fountain. More reflections. Heaven knows how Dick will edit all these together, but he is anxious to show us the rushes before the final version, for our approval.

Finally free from the cameras (the BBC commending the children on their extraordinary patience, good humour and lack of affectation), we were dropped back at the poshy school and 'Provincial House' of Santa Clara, where Sr Maria Rosa (English and Music teacher with a lush American accent, which Pedro mimicked to her great amusement) took us to the organ loft to regale us with English carols(!) and then escorted us to her class of 15-year-olds, all agog to meet the author and composer of *Go Tell Everyone*, the best-known of Bert's songs. He wrote it in the sixties. This they rendered, to the accompaniment of two skilled guitarists, with enormous gusto, if strange enunciation. But they knew the words better than Bert himself. Bert translated his *Polenta Song* into Spanish and brought the house down. Finally, Blanca's *Oh Daddy* melted everyone.

An enormous lunch of delicately curried rice and chicken,
and a farewell consisting of all the community entering
the parlour with three guitars to sing to us. What a send
off from these most gentle and generous of nuns. And
what memories it brought back of this same parlour nine
years ago!

I started the new year of 1975 in a bedsit in West London, travelling each day to teach a group of disturbed
youngsters. I can't say I found it very easy, but I was
perfectly content, with a sense of anticipation about the
future. I'm very lucky that, by temperament, I think
positively when a challenge is there. I can't remember
ever looking back and having second thoughts about my
decision to leave the convent. There was a new beginning ahead. I was thirty-seven. Plenty of time for another life adventure.

I love London. It was good to have time and the
freedom to go where I liked, when I liked. One of the
first things I did was to visit Bert Richards, my old
teacher and friend. He had been a tower of strength
during my final year in the convent because he too was
in a position of uncertainty about his vocation in the
Church. I knew that he could understand, from his own
experience, my questionings and uncertainties. Our
friendship was not without problems. Neither of us
wanted to be distracted from the original reasons for
our re-thinking about our roles in the Church.

Several months after I left the convent Bert made his
decision to ask for laicisation from the priesthood. It
was a difficult decision because he felt so responsible to
the many hundreds of priest, nun and lay students who
had looked to him for support. He was a well-loved
teacher, whose students admired the way he had made

the Scriptures come alive. But the pressure put on him by the Cardinal had become too much. After the forced departure from Corpus Christi College, he had been kept in a kind of limbo. His application for a teaching post at a Catholic theological college was blocked by the Cardinal, and he was told he was no longer to preach. He was not attached to a parish, in fact he was only able to live by the generosity of family and friends. (Catholic priests are kept by their parish. Bert didn't have one.)

The Cardinal was deeply shocked at Bert's decision to leave. In spite of his doubts about Bert's orthodoxy, he was genuinely appreciative of his loyalty and sincerity as a priest of the Westminster Diocese. Bert made the official announcement after he had found a post as New Testament lecturer in a college in Norwich. His statement made it clear that he was resigning with sadness.

I am announcing my resignation from the Roman Catholic priesthood because it has been made progressively clearer to me over the past three years that as a priest I am not free to teach theology in any Roman Catholic establishment in this country. During my twenty-nine years in the priesthood, I have tried sincerely to follow what I regard as my vocation — to make the results of theological scholarship available to teachers and students, by lecturing and writing, in as moderate and constructive a way as possible. I regret that this is no longer acceptable to my superiors.

I have been very happy in the priesthood, which has given me countless opportunities for helping people, and in so doing of receiving help myself. It is my loss that the present choice has been, as I see it, forced on me. I intend to remain a Catholic, and I am confident that my future work in a non-Catholic College of Education will offer me opportunities at present denied me in my own Church.

H.J. Richards.

In the days that followed Bert received hundreds of letters. He knew he would receive total support and love from his family, but he was surprised by the volume and warmth of the love he received from his former colleagues and students. They wrote from around the world, letter after letter echoing understanding, admiration and encouragement. 'Wherever your path leads, the love of those you have related to in Christ will be with you. You are much loved! Keep that guitar playing! God keep you in the very centre of his heart.' Many were sad at the loss they felt, but still wrote words of encouragement: 'I weep for you and for us — and for our poor Church. It was not the authority of your priesthood that made your teaching valid for me but your obvious, deep commitment as a fellow human being.' There were kind letters from priest colleagues: 'One's regard for you is strengthened by seeing you act on your convictions.' Another priest wrote: 'Maybe it is you who have the courage and the rest of us who have not.'

There were a handful of letters from Catholics who disapproved, like the contemplative nun who wrote: 'I still feel you would do more for the Church by your daily Mass than any amount of lecturing or writing.' But another nun felt able to write, 'If a really nice person comes along, Bert, get married and at least have someone with whom you can really share.' Someone else wrote, 'If you should follow in the footsteps of your notable predecessors and marry, I, for one, should dance at your wedding.'

Six months later there was a wedding to dance at! Bert and I saw much of each other over the summer, enjoying each other's company with increasing enthusiasm. We had such a lot to share and such similar ideals about the future Church of which we wanted to be a part. It's strange how often people presume ex-nuns and priests turn their backs on the Church altogether. Some have. But most of us haven't. It wasn't very long before we realised that we were looking forward to spending every free moment together. We decided that the future was ours to share together. Our concern for each other had grown from friendship into love.

We are both blessed with wonderful families. Bert's parents, so proud of their priest son, had died. They would probably have found our decision difficult. But his brother and sisters welcomed me with warmth and generosity. I'm quite certain it was difficult for them to readjust to his new status. But they did everything to show us love and practical help. We had, after all, little material security to launch into married life. With great joy, and blissfully ignorant of monetary matters, we visited Norwich to plan for the future.

Bert's residential teaching post at a College of Education in Norwich was settled. So I also applied for a teaching post at a school for maladjusted children in the city. I was amazed to get the job, and we happily set about house-hunting. We hadn't a penny in the bank and were ignorant about mortgages. Yet somehow we returned to London with my job and a house under our belts. We liked the first house we saw, a small Victorian terrace. The owner wanted to sell quickly and we, as first-time buyers, had no reason to hold him up. He must have thought it strange that this was to be our first home. Bert was fifty-three! We had no difficulty in getting a mortgage because of our teaching prospects.

At the beginning of September I moved into our house, and Bert moved into his college. At the very time we had decided to marry Bert's elder sister had sadly died. The family immediately gave us the contents of her home. In what strange ways things work out.

We settled down in our new jobs and our new city with great ease, spurred on by anticipation of our Christmas wedding. We set the date and started the plans. There was one difficulty. For some unknown reason Bert's laicisation papers had never come from Rome. We needed them for our church wedding. With less than a month to go we decided that a letter had to be written to Cardinal Heenan telling him of our plans. We had wanted to avoid this, knowing that he would immediately accuse Bert of leaving the priesthood, 'in order to get married', a reason which the Cardinal considered was unworthy. If he thought this, he would not even begin to explore the real issues.

We don't know if he ever read the letter. He died suddenly on the day he should have received it. A few days later an anxious phone call from his assistant bishop, Bishop Butler, explained that the Cardinal had never sent off Bert's letter of resignation to Rome. Perhaps he had hoped for a change of mind. The bishop assured us he would do everything he could to get the permission through in time for the planned day. He did so, with a day to spare!

Bert's lifelong friend, Monsignor Pat Murphy O'Connor, married us in St John's Catholic Cathedral, in the presence of our close family and a few friends. Good Bishop Butler sent us a congratulatory telegram. We honeymooned over Christmas in Tenerife, and wondered at how easily and naturally we welcomed the physical expression of our love.

It seemed obvious that if we were to have a family, we

had to start moving smartly. We soon discovered that it wasn't going to be that easy. I had a series of early miscarriages and paid a number of fruitless visits to gynaecologists. I even took a year off school, but that didn't help either. So I returned to teaching, this time to Notre Dame Catholic High School. Meanwhile we enquired about adoption, but discovered we were far too old to be considered. Slowly we gave up the dream of having a family, and settled for the great happiness our marriage was already giving us. When Jonathan Dimbleby changed everything.

One evening in 1979 I turned on the television and by chance saw a programme he was presenting from Colombia. It was the International Year of the Child and his programme was highlighting the poverty of children in the Third World. Within moments he had me riveted.

Dimbleby was following the progress of several French and American couples who were in Bogotà to conclude adoption arrangements. The sight of those happy couples being matched with abandoned babies spoke to me loud and clear. I dashed to the study and whipped Bert away from the exam papers he was marking. By the end of the programme our minds were made up. We could at least try to adopt a Colombian baby. If the French and the Americans could do it, why not us?

I went to bed that night wondering why I had not thought of this before. After all Bogota was a city already etched on my mind and heart, and surely the Poor Child Jesus Sisters would help us. So began a year of excitement, expectation, anxiety, frustration — and finally sheer joy.

We wrote to Jonathan Dimbleby. The producer of his programme phoned us and gave us the address of a Children's Home in Bogota. Of course we also contacted my Sisters there, through Sister Ursula in London. They agreed to intercede for us. We spent months filling in forms and getting them translated into Spanish. All along we were guided and helped by a sympathetic social worker from our County Hall, Mrs Wiggins, who vetted us and gave approval. But then came a series of hiccups.

First the children's home in Bogota accepted us on their list but could promise nothing for at least two years. Then our government presented a bill in parliament to change the immigration laws. We didn't know if this would make overseas adoptions impossible. We wrote to the Home Office several times, and each time a computer reply sent us the same form (already completed by us long ago) with their compliments. Our appeals to local MPs for information met with uncertain replies. One evening I felt so frustrated at the lack of information that I sat down and wrote to Mrs Thatcher herself. Her Downing Street office replied immediately on her behalf, reassuring us that it was safe to go ahead with plans.

But then came a more worrying setback. Bert had to attend an annual medical inspection in Harley Street. He was a guinea pig patient of a specialist in cholesterol problems. It had been established some years previously that he had a strange reaction to normal drugs for high cholesterol levels. So he was given a free annual checkup as he tried out various medicines. He happened to mention a slight tummy pain and was immediately referred for investigation to our own hospital in Norwich. Within a few weeks he was admitted and a cancer operation took place on the very day medical forms arrived from Colombia. (One morning whilst Bert was still in hospital I received a phone call from the Mount of Olives, Jerusalem. It was Muhammad, the camel driver whose home Bert had visited many times. 'I hear my brother is in hospital. How is he? Can I help pay his hospital fees? He is my brother. I am worried and want to help him.' I assured him that our NHS — this was 1980 — was still in good shape.) Fortunately the cancer was caught in its earliest stages, and Bert recovered remarkably quickly. He was pronounced fit, given a clean medical prognosis and we were ready to continue the search for our baby.

It was then that my sisters in Bogota came up trumps. We had asked them to withdraw our papers from the Children's Home and seek another way of finding us a child. They agreed, but warned us in May 1980 that the Colombian Government was tightening up its adoption procedure. In order to control overseas applications they were quite rightly channelling all adoptions through a single state-controlled agency. Private adoptions were out. So things did not look too good.

I had just made the mental shift of accepting the failure of all our plans when a letter arrived on the mat. It was a Thursday morning July 10. It announced so simply, 'Your twins have arrived'.

I went to school in a daze. Twins, a boy and a girl, were waiting for us in Colombia. We knew nothing about them yet. Bert took the day off from his university and tried to get through by phone to Bogota for more news. On the way home from school I went into Mothercare to buy a dozen nappies. I felt I was walking on air. I wanted to tell everyone that at long last I had reason to shop there. Ever since my first miscarriage I had found Mothercare a source of heavy-hearted sadness. I never liked walking near the shop. Now I was to become a frequent dreamy-eyed visitor, enthusing over baby powder and gripe water.

I went into school the next day and told my class that

we had just phoned Bogota and heard the children's names: Pedro and Blanca. I told them that we thought they really needed English names, and we had chosen Benjamin and Rebecca. The whole class erupted. 'No, no,' they insisted. 'They must always be Pedro and Blanca.' They were right of course.

As the day for our journey halfway across the world drew nearer, we checked and re-checked our papers. Everything seemed in order: the medical papers, the birth and marriage certificates, the bank statements, the Home Office adoption forms, the official Notary's stamp of approval — the papers probably weighed more than the babies did. We had to ignore one Home Office instruction — it clashed with the reality of life in the Third World. We were told to wait until the Home Office cleared our papers before travelling. We were warned it could take six months. Our babies were waiting for us. It was a struggle to keep them alive in Colombia. We needed to travel at once.

Family, friends and neighbours kept calling with gifts: a baby bath, blankets, teddy bears and piles of nappies. My class made two enormous soft toys, and a mobile for the nursery. I was indescribably happy. I spent hours shopping, savouring the joy of choosing baby clothes, and bathtime soaps and oils.

On August 2 we flew from London to Bogota. It was almost unreal, travelling for sixteen hours in order to reach the babies who were to make our family complete. The final hours of waiting seemed the longest of all. When we arrived at the convent, Santa Clara's, the babies were not there. They were at the clinic. We were told to go and have a much needed rest. It was strange — back in one of my convents, everything familiar as though I had hardly been away. But I was resting at the side of my husband!

They woke us half an hour later to usher us into the convent parlour. Twenty nuns lined the walls, agog to see our reaction. Then the door opened and our babies were brought in. Sister Martha Lucia carried a tiny bundle in a blue blanket; Sister Claudia Angelica carried Blanca in a yellow blanket. All we could see were tiny tufts of black hair, and two enormous pairs of shining black eyes.

I took Pedro into my arms and Bert gently lifted Blanca into his. A tiny hand shot out, plucked his sunglasses from his shirt pocket, and dropped them on to the floor. 'That's my girl', he said. I hugged my little blue bundle and hoped that the love I felt for Pedro and his sister would reach his heart. I can never forget this moment in the convent parlour with the community gathered to share our happiness.

We had to bring Pedro and Blanca back to this room today. It is like walking on holy ground.

7 A FAMILY

DIARY August 7

Today was an important one. The BBC took us and
Sister Martha Lucia to Bosa, the suburban school where
the sisters had first nurtured Blanca and Pedro in a
converted classroom before handing them over to us. The
violent contrast between the dilapidated and ramshackle
village, with its desperate, dusty, pot-holed roads, and the
oasis of flowers, tarmac and cleanliness beyond the school
gates, where the sisters offer a free education to the
village children.

It was not only the beautiful surroundings. The warm
welcome given to all comers (groups of visitors, drivers,
friends, parents are always to be seen being fed and
watered in a dozen different parlours) — this has
obviously an enormous part to play in the education of
the children here. They looked an extraordinarily joyful
lot — and crowded round us to giggle and try out their
English.

Filming was rather tedious, especially since the sun was
desperately hot (compared with yesterday's overcast
coolness), and takes and retakes and close-up and voice
shots were the order of the day.

We had a sequence in the classroom with Pedro and
Blanca sitting in a geography class with other nine-year
olds; a sequence where I explained to our two the 3ft
appliqué I had made in 1981 with a dozen vignettes of
life in Bosa; a sequence where we walked in the garden
and found again the cowshed where the cows had been
milked straight onto the dry skins of Pedro and Blanca;
and finally a sequence in the classroom which had been

the children's first nursery, where we had first accepted the terrifying responsibility of looking after them.

In between, a fine lunch for the whole TV crew and us, including, strangely, fried bananas wrapped in streaky bacon. A tiring but highly enjoyable day, packed with memories. Extraordinary to look at the children now with the memories of their fragile beginning awakened so vividly. I realise how much I love this place.

On the way back in the BBC van through miles of shanty towns during the rush hour, Pedro remarked to Bert, 'Difficult to survive here, Dad, I imagine.' But he and Blanca both admitted to feeling much more at home in these surroundings than in the embattled fortress on the other side of the city where we had spent the first night.

A light supper and then away to pack for a week in the country. It will be good, if sweatier, getting off this plateau into the lowlands. But it will be hard leaving Sister Martha Lucia behind.

Our very first meeting with Pedro and Blanca was brief. We had to stay on in the Provincial House of Santa Clara to be near the British Embassy, the lawyer and the Children's Department, while the children returned to their temporary nursery in the suburb convent in Bosa. There they were being looked after by the headmistress, Sister Claudia Angelica, who had been responsible for finding the twins in the first place.

Meanwhile we were warmly welcomed in Bogota by the provincial superior — the sister responsible for all the Poor Child Jesus sisters in Colombia — Mother Teresina. We liked her immediately. Motherliness incarnate. Warm moist eyes, turning to laughter and tears alternately. She told us the story of the children's early months. It was a hazy story. It didn't help that Mother Teresina, a German, did not speak any English.

Fortunately I had learnt some German in the convent, so I could understand something. Bert did much better.

We understood that the twins' birth caused a great problem in their family. Delfina, their mother, had six children already when she became pregnant by another man. Her distraught husband seemed to have abandoned her, as did their father. Something went wrong at the hospital birth which left her paralysed and unable to return home for four months. It was left to their four-year-old half sister to care for them during those first months. Heaven knows how she managed it.

Sister Claudia Angelica's mother and sister lived in the children's village of La Argentina. When they heard of the plight of the little twins up in the mountains (the family home lay out of the village), they remembered that the nuns had friends in England who wanted to adopt a baby. Sister Claudia Angelica took the long journey to the village, and went with her mother and the mayor's wife out to the struggling family. They found Pedro hours away from death. He was lying in the corner of the dark room, huddled up, dehydrated and covered with mildew. He had been left to die. Blanca was a little stronger and her mother wept at the realisation that she had no means to help her survive either. Sadly she agreed to let them be adopted and signed a form to give her permission legally. The twins were rushed away from her as Pedro needed urgent medical care. He weighed only 4 lbs and was probably about seven months old. Blanca was a little stronger, weighing nearly 7 lbs.

When we heard the story we understood why the Santa Clara community had buzzed around us, anxious to see our reaction to such poor little mites. It explained the sad little face that gazed out of the blue blanket. The dark shadows under the big eyes didn't hide the memory of those starving days. His serious little expression moved us to tears.

Mother Teresina explained that the community were also a little anxious that we may not really have wanted to adopt Indian children. That this could worry them had never entered our minds. But one thing did enter my mind. I didn't know if the sisters were at all aware of my background. And I felt I was cheating them if I remained silent about it.

I asked to see Mother Teresina on my own. In my poor German I asked her if she knew that I had once been Sister Clare in Finchley and Southam. Her reply was an enormous hug, tears in her eyes and whispered words, 'Natürlich, natürlich'. Then she said, 'When the community was anxious that you may refuse such poor children, I knew that these were just the ones you would want. I know that you have the heart of Mother Clare.' The next day Mother Teresina took me to Andrès Fey, to the seat under the tree, to remind me of my letter asking to come out to Bogota. 'The time is right for you to come here now', she said. 'Pedro and Blanca need you.'

We spent the next days toing and froing between Santa Clara's and their Bosa nursery, a classroom emptied and refurnished with three old bedsteads.

Some days we sat with the children for hours in their quiet room, watching and learning from the love with which Sister Claudia Angelica and Sister Martha Lucia massaged their little limbs. The children lay motionless on the beds listening first to the music on a tape machine by their pillows, later to Bert softly singing and playing the guitar, Pedro ever pensive, and Blanca fascinated by his pipe smoke.

We went with them when they were carried down the garden to get their Cleopatra treatment from the loveable farm sister. She sat by the cow and milked directly on to their bare bodies in turn, rubbing the milk into their scaly, scabies-infected skin.

Gradually, sensitively, the Sisters handed the babies over to our care. We learnt to change nappies, rock to sleep and feed — not without difficulty in a country where water is a problem and milk powder instructions are in Spanish. The children seemed to grow visibly before our eyes. We had brought with us Mothercare baby-carriers, and they took to them delightedly. We wrapped them up warm against the sharp Bosa wind and took them round the school grounds for their first outings.

There came the day when I was to sleep with them for the first time. I was not a little nervous. There was no room for Bert in the nursery, so he was given a room next door. Finally after many instructions I went to bed. I wrote in the 1980 diary, 'A very disturbed night! Bed hard as rocks (on wooden boards) and Pedro snores.' Blanca was already sleeping most of the way through the night. Pedro needed a midnight feed which I managed creeping around in the semi-dark, making up his bottle from a flask of hot water. I was anxious to get it ready quickly before his cries woke up Blanca.

I had been shown how to bind him up in a kind of swaddling bands, necessary because of the bitterly cold mountain nights. He snuggled down and went to sleep. I felt triumphant.

At 4.00 am he woke again. I changed him, fed him and wrapped up the swaddling bands, and put him back on his bed. I lay down too and when he seemed sleepy I turned to look at Blanca who was still sleeping peacefully. I was startled by a little poke in the back. Pedro had unwound his arm and rolled over to touch me. I looked at him and he gave the flicker of a smile. It was the first moment that I really felt I was mother to them. I cried as I took Pedro in my arms and we watched the dawn come up together. But oh, what a mistake! He naturally demanded that cuddle every morning after that. Well no, it wasn't a mistake. I never minded getting up in the night to cuddle and whisper to them. Those quiet night times were far too precious ever to regret. Later, at home, Bert and I took turns to feed Pedro at night. It was sheer bliss to feel the contented little body close to my own, sucking blissfully and pinching at my arm with every suck. The loving look he rewarded us with was worth the morning's tiredness. I was sorry that Blanca didn't need these night-time trysts.

So we came and went to Bosa, regretting every moment we couldn't be with the babies. But Claudia Angelica and Martha Lucia loved having them so much it was bearable to leave them behind. Meanwhile in Bogota, Sister Virgilia was pressing us to see something of the town, and we reluctantly let her fuss around and show us the sights. In between we spent much time negotiating with the lawyer and the British Consul. Both were efficient, kind, and full of encouragement. The lawyer was moreover honest. By sheer coincidence we found that his wife worked for a government-approved children's home, and so we were able to have Pedro and Blanca swiftly and officially listed for an overseas adoption.

Fonseca, the lawyer, told us that the time the adoption took to be completed depended entirely on the weekly selection of judges for adoption cases. He knew the judges who made life difficult, and he simply withdrew applications at the last moment if one of these judges was appointed. 'How long could it take?' we asked. 'One week, five weeks, ten weeks — depending.'

When news came that the judge would be picked that day, Fonseca asked for prayers to get the right one first time. 'Which saint?' asked Sister Virgilia. 'All of them.'

Virgilia opened her cupboard to reveal twenty-five statues for all occasions. 'The black one is best' she said, and produced St Martin de Porres — with a record of favours glued to his bottom. When the news came that it was the right judge first time, Virgilia knew that her saint had done it again!

An important Bogota visit was to the *Bienestar Familiar*, the Welfare Office where we had to sign papers to complete the adoption process, and establish that the children's medical papers were in order. Next we had to apply for their passports. Then we had to search the banks to find dollars to pay our legal fees. We discovered that we could only get dollars by paying 8% costs. Bert courteously declined. Later Fonseca put us on to a private operator who did a 5% deal in the convent parlour.

When news came that the passports were ready, Mother Teresina moved us into the convent infirmary so that we could bring the twins over from Bosa for the last days of our stay. Sad farewells from the Bosa community and children who had taken the babies to their hearts. Thank goodness Sister Martha Lucia came with us. I needed her help. Claudia Angelica and her mother, Beatrix, often came over to see us.

It was a strange start to our life as a family. There we were, Bert included, sleeping inside the convent enclosure. It was probably the first time the Sisters had opened their enclosure doors to lay people. We had a constant stream of nunnish visitors, the babies responding with appropriate gurgles and grins. Martha Lucia was up with me late into the nights and appeared at the crack of dawn to help with nappies and feeds. Pedro cried a great deal, desperate for food and entertainment. Blanca seemed altogether more self-possessed and content, happy with her own company for hours on end.

By now we were only awaiting clearance from the Home Office for immigration. The Embassy was negotiating for us, with messages sent back and forth in the diplomatic bag. Bert whiled away the time sketching and composing lullabies — which the stream of visitors seemed to enjoy more than the twins. The daily improvement in the children's health was a bit of a miracle. Blanca's general contentment was a joy to behold. So was Pedro's fierce determination — presumably the only reason that he had survived at all. I could never quite get over the look of bliss in their faces as they fed regularly, and got a disastrous fit of the giggles towards the end as their eyes lost focus, rolled about in utter abandon, and finally glazed over.

I finally glazed over myself when flight after flight home had to be cancelled as our final permission from the Home Office to travel failed to appear. Bert told me to take a siesta after lunch. I fell asleep instantly, leaving him to entertain two very lively and wideawake babies. By 2.30 Bert was nearly prostrate himself with weariness, and as I woke up to feed them he gratefully took my place on the bed. Not for long. Within minutes the Embassy was phoning to say our immigration clearance had arrived. No more sleep! With minutes to spare we phoned Air France to confirm our provisional seats and ordered plenty of milk. Since the Embassy staff wanted to see Blanca and Pedro before we left, we hurriedly dressed them up and dashed over by taxi just before the Embassy closed for the weekend. There we received the permission in a simple letter, unauthenticated, unstamped, unphotocopied, no charge. What a contrast to the hours of bureaucratic queueing up we had done for Colombian documents.

Back at Santa Clara's we booked a phone-call to England to announce our arrival at Heathrow. We hesitantly asked Mother Teresina about our bill. She said there wasn't one. We mentioned plane flights for the children from Neiva, food, hospital bills, medicines, nappies galore, laundry, phone-calls — not to mention our three-and-a-half week bed and board. She wouldn't hear of it. This was all part of the work of the Congregation. We were part of the Congregation.

A constant stream of nuns came to say good-bye to the twins, around whom the whole life of the Congregation in Bogotá had revolved for nearly two months. We took them to Compline that evening, and again the next day rose with the community at 4.30 am to attend a 5.00 am Mass. The whole province were having an away-day in the sun, a monthly get-together to relax from their demanding work. By 6.00 am when they were all boarding the bus, we had Pedro and Blanca looking washed and shining for everyone to have a last ogle, chuck under the chin and poke in the ribs. They bore it all with commendable tolerance. But it was a very weepy goodbye to Teresina, Martha Lucia and Claudia Angelica.

Virgilia was left behind to see us off to the airport. We hoped she would leave us at the Air France desk. Not a bit of it. In her true style, Wiggles (as we had come to call her) marched ahead of the queue, demanding immediate attention. She refused to let Bert hold the passports or tickets or papers, and waving them high in the air frogmarched us through the airport tax, check-in, passport control, customs and emigration. One had the distinct feeling from the faces of the officials that they knew her well. She came unstuck when Bert managed a word of French to an Air France official. He gathered that they wanted us to wait in a private lounge to be taken aboard the plane at the last moment. Bert insisted on obeying them. Wiggles argued that she knew best, but finally caved in by going off with a German businessman for a free coffee in the Airport Director's office.

She appeared in time for us to say our (genuinely) grateful goodbyes, as did Claudia Angelica's mother and sister. We were taken out by car to the plane, given seats just behind the first class passengers, and received first-class treatment throughout the flight. With one 'air-cot' and a spare seat beside us made into a little bed, the two of them fed contentedly and slept like angels. Blanca had eyes for a charming steward, who waited on her every need, asking if he could warm a fresh 'bertelle' every time he passed.

So we arrived in England, with Air France stewardesses constantly on hand to carry our luggage so that we could manage the twins. We had been warned at the Embassy that the Chief Immigration Officer had the right to refuse anyone entry. We saw ourselves through customs and then had to return to join the immigration queues. The lady at the desk queried the children's medical certificate, indicating that it might not be sufficiently detailed. I had my No. 10 Downing Street letter on hand, just in case of problems! It wasn't needed. When the Chief Officer arrived he took one look at the sleeping pair, said, 'Jolly good show' and stamped their passports with 'Indefinite Stay'.

With a sigh of relief and indescribable joy we walked out to the waiting, expectant crowds and looked for my mother and brother who had come to take us home. We had gone out a couple, we had come back a family.

8 GROWING UP

DIARY August 8

All that talk of 'off to the countryside' sounds rather thin
in retrospect: today was a series of disasters which made
one speculate again whether things really happen by
conspiracy or by cock-up.

The planned start at 9.00 inevitably became 9.30 —
only to be told that one van had to have an extra bench
fixed. This meant unloading all the TV equipment
(including ten crates of mineral water for 'the wilds') and
reloading after. Meanwhile the other van had to go off to
buy sunhats for everyone (!). By the time this was done,
and we were waiting for each other at two different places
for three-quarters of an hour, we finally got on the main
road south at 11.30. Talk about *Kolumbianische Zeit!*

Through miles of urban sprawl. The whole of Bogota
— and presumably the whole of the country — continues
as nine years ago to be a vast construction site. People
live in groundfloors as upper stories are being added.
Road works everywhere.

Finally the open road, through the Andes foothills,
sometimes snaking among them, but finally in the
broad glacial plain of the Magdalena river. The
reduced altitude made breathing easier — in a sense.
But the increased heat made sitting by the open van
window rather like having a fan heater on a table in
front of you, turned on at full strength, only blowing at
60 mph instead of 6. Rather exhausting. Banana
plantations, with coffee growing in their shade, cotton
fields, stalls selling exotic fruits. Large roadside stones
every mile or so, painted white, bearing the inscription,

'Christ is coming soon.' Bert remarked, 'Promise or threat?'

After a lunch stop among a clutch of country clubs, each with its own swimming pool, we finally made our overnight stop at Neiva at 5 pm. The two van loads of sweaty humanity (us four, the BBC team of five, the interpreter, Mauricio, Sister Claudia Angelica's mother Beatrix, who is accompanying us on this leg, and the two van drivers) all tumbled out into the Diaz family home, a sprawling colonial house with a vast tiled reception area already filled with cousins and in-laws and half a dozen noisy children. More people arrived over the hours, adding more children to the chaos.

More aimless chaos during the hours that followed, with nobody quite knowing what to expect. Fruit juice was drunk in quantities. It was breathlessly hot. Dick Meadows, our producer, was chary of allowing any beer to his crew.

The immediate object was to film the arrival of Sister Claudia Angelica, the nun originally responsible for finding the children up in the remote Andes. She was coming from miles away in Supiá, near Medellin. She had turned down the BBC offer of flying her as far as Bogota or Neiva (no doubt on the grounds of poverty) and was making a fifteen-hour bus journey, with several changes. A tricky undertaking since each area runs its own service, and without any attempt to organise connections there is no common timetable. Throughout the evening various members of the crew went haring round the town making enquiries. It emerged that a bus was due hourly, at 5.30 or so, at 6.30 or so, at 7.30 or so. . . . We hoped to film her coming off one of these buses, and being greeted by us.

When hour after hour nothing happened, in spite of Mauricio shouting above the hubbub through his portable executive phone to all and sundry; and our children were getting tetchy because they couldn't communicate with the dozen children who wanted to play with them, and could see the promised swim at a

Country Club slowly disappearing; and the evening air, even outdoors, grew more and more humid — Dick finally called it off at 8.15, saying we would reconstruct something in the morning. If Claudia Angelica arrived at all! Only to find his two drivers were even more fed up than the rest of us, and had taken off! It took half an hour to locate them, and the BBC crew went off to their hotel.

It was now 9.00 pm, and M's phone had finally afforded us the information that the Country Club was off. So he rushed us off to a restaurant where only Colombian food is served, insisting. Nice place, open air by the river. But impossibly loud piped music, and the food took an hour to come. Speciality chicken tasty enough, but Mauricio finished it in five minutes complaining it was badly done. While we finished ours, he continued conversing with his toy phone, without getting any further information about Claudia Angelica. Gloomy conversation trying to dissuade us from venturing further into the mountains to visit the children's birthplace of La Argentina, where they are 'all thieves, desperadoes and kidnappers'. So a gloomy finish to the day, still with no news of C.A.

To confirm the fact that we were finishing the day on a downbeat, we discovered when we finally unpacked, that much of the Rice Crispies had tipped into the bottom of the plastic bag, and got rather embroiled with the ripe passion fruit, severely sludging the bottom of the gin bottle. Much washing up down the loo, where the bits of passion fruit refused to go down the drain. And so to bed.

If our journey back to the children's first home started with a series of minor disasters, it was not unlike the first day of our journey back home nine years ago. We arrived in Heathrow with no luggage. Wiggles' fussing at the airport had successfully prevented Bert from checking-in his own luggage. It wasn't on our plane. So we had to stay overnight in Knebworth with Mum and

Dad, and return for the luggage. Mind you, this was highly successful since it introduced the children to the family and gave us a break as everyone lent a hand.

Monday (Bank Holiday) we moved on to Norwich, wondering what our re-designed kitchen would look like — we had left it in the hands of a builder. Disaster. He was uncertain about final details and had left walls bare, lino and carpet up, ugly holes everywhere, dust and dirt inches thick. The babies were quickly introduced to their (comparatively) dustless bedroom, while I, Bert and Mum (staying a few days which was a brainwave) swept, scrubbed, moved, cut lino and carpet to allow supper to be cooked and bottles prepared.

We hadn't been home a few hours before Pedro cried and cried. I had only just fed him, so I tried changing his nappy, cuddling him, walking up and down. Nothing would stop his crying. I phoned the doctor. 'Why don't you try giving him more milk?' she asked, after she had examined everything. I did so and he stopped instantly, settled down and slept. He was just hungry. I felt foolish!

But our hiccups ended there. Everything went from better to better. Weeks later the clinic nurse asked if I had had my doubts and baby-blues yet. 'Every adopting mother gets them' she said. I never did. I have loved every moment of mothering Pedro and Blanca. Those earliest days at home getting to know them were perhaps the happiest days I have ever experienced.

We began the proceedings for adoption under English law on the day after returning to Norwich. Everything went smoothly. Three and a half months later we attended the Family Court to complete the adoption. It was December 19 1980. We had the most lovely first Christmas as a real family.

Meanwhile I invited my former class at Notre Dame

High School to help me prepare for the children's baptism — the Christian celebration of life as God's gift. Pedro and Blanca were welcomed into our local Christian community in the school hall. Blanca cried quite a bit, but stopped immediately Bert picked her up, to the delight of the schoolchildren. Pedro watched and listened, wide-eyed, at the ceremony and the singing. The pupils welcomed the pair of them with toys, with a requested song on local radio, and even with their first deposit in a building society.

I had to take the children to the clinic every week for many months. The nurses and doctors were anxious to monitor their progress because they had never seen children like this recovering from severe malnutrition. We watched as they slowly made up their weight and as their muscles grew stronger. Pedro could not lift his head when we first arrived home. I was blissfully ignorant that this signalled a possibility of retardation. It never occurred to me that the hardship of their early months may have caused irreparable damage.

At first the doctors suspected we had mistimed their true birthday. They thought that the twins were much younger than the birth certificates stated. What they were quite sure about was that Sister Martha Lucia had saved Pedro's life by holding him for those first vital hours. Her body warmth kept him alive. So did her love. Many a night as I tucked Pedro up I wished I had Martha Lucia near me to share the wonder of seeing him grow healthy and happy. The doctors finally revised their first thoughts and agreed that their age was about right.

When the childen were three years old we had to attend the clinic for the usual child development tests. There was a new doctor in attendance and he had read the children's notes before the testing. 'Well, I never did!' he exclaimed. 'They have both scored on the good side of average.' When we seemed surprised at his exclamation, he told us that he had expected Pedro to be quite retarded and possibly Blanca too. I had always supposed that loving and feeding the children and spending every moment with them, playing and talking and sharing our whole selves would compensate for any early hardship. I obviously guessed correctly.

Of course the children changed our lives dramatically. I was a stay-at-home mother, and I found the full-time demands of motherhood more exhausting, more exciting and more fulfilling than anything I had ever known. Bert took to fatherhood instantly. His study lost its sacredness from day one. We had a soft baby ball suspended from the ceiling at the side of his desk. Pedro or Blanca would sit for hours with him, swinging the ball and gurgling. The tape recorder on the desk stopped playing quiet music, and began to record first words, then baby chatter, then songs. His desk drawers were soon taken over by fat crayola crayons, favourite cars and precious 'scribbles'. Nine years later there are still toys to be mended sitting on the corner of his desk, and now Pedro's drum sticks and percussion music sit by Bert's latest manuscript and Blanca's guitar hangs alongside his, awaiting the daily practice with Dad advising. Blanca has, of course, never ceased to be 'his girl'. Her independence and warmth combine to give her an endearing nature. Bert has always revelled in her challenging, strong-willed approach to life.

From early on we were both staggered by the children's grasp of the deepest realities. It has made us revise many of our religious concepts. We already realised that our grasp of theology was going to change at our first Christmas. During the morning church service

Bert had Pedro on his knee. All during the Mass Pedro burbled what sounded like his first word, 'abba'. It was a moving reminder that we were celebrating the birth of a boy who would later address God as his 'Abba' (Father). I'm sure all babies burble 'abba' as a first word, but for Bert, Pedro's 'abba' signalled a whole new understanding of the Fatherhood of God. From those first days my experience of becoming a mother has given me a new appreciation of the Motherhood of God. But it has given me too a firmer grasp of the basic Christian doctrine of Incarnation.

As a nun I spent many hours meditating on the presence of God in the world. I have to admit that the busy life of a mother has given me a greater understanding of this reality. I used to think, because I was taught to, that I could really only get to know God by spending hours in silent prayer. Today I no longer see Christian prayer in terms of grabbing an hour here or there to absent myself from daily family tasks. God isn't remote or difficult to reach. The joy, love and laughter that Pedro and Blanca have brought to Bert and me bring us constantly into God's presence.

I often think what a great blessing motherhood is for a Christian because it makes a life of prayer so much easier. We can pray all the time. 'God is love, and anyone who lives in love lives in God, and God lives in him' (1 John 4:6). I don't think we even need to use the word God in our prayers. The loving is sufficient. And with children there is an abundance of it. I am deeply aware of God's presence when Blanca hugs me and says, 'Oh Mummy, I do love you, and I love Daddy and I love Pedro and I love me.' God is the love between us and I feel him in her bear-hug and I see him in Pedro's sparkling eyes.

I remember revising my idea of prayer one night

77

when I was sitting up with a very spotty, uncomfortable little Pedro. He had caught chicken-pox from his sister. As I was dabbing on calamine lotion at 3.00 am I was aware that my neighbour Ros was possibly doing the same to one of her chicken-poxed children. And there were probably hundreds of mums and dads up in Norwich alone, like my friend Doreen, feeding her new baby, or the mothers giving doses of calpol or puffs of ventolin inhalers to their sick children. I knew old Miss Pond, my neighbour, was likely to be awake too. I thought of us all as a community of prayer, joining in with the nuns and monks of religious orders who get up in the night to praise God in formal prayer.

I learnt from Blanca that prayer is simply holding on to God. When she was five she fractured her elbow. She had to spend four weeks in hospital, flat on her back, an enormous metal pin through her arm in traction. I daily grew in admiration of my daughter. She longed to go home. She couldn't, but she didn't complain. She wanted to sit upright. She couldn't, but she didn't complain. She wanted the elaborate toys other children were receiving. We couldn't afford them, but she didn't complain. By week three all she wanted was a pillow for her tired head. She wasn't given one, but she didn't complain. By the final week she had no more 'wants', as long as we were near to hold her hand. I learned more from this experience than from any sermon, that it is possible to let go of everything as long as we hold on to God. And perhaps it takes suffering to make us take the first step.

It is experiences like these that have made me question the wisdom of having regular Sunday sermons from male celibate priests. Of course they have something to share with us, but it is *so* limited. Once when the children were quite small a priest friend came to stay with us. He was rather intense and very aware that *he* was the man of God. He offered to give his blessing to anyone and anything at the drop of a hat. Bert and I could just about cope with this but the children couldn't — rightly so. When he surveyed Pedro and Blanca, scrubbed and pyjama-ed and ready for bed and offered once again to bless them, Pedro whispered to me — I hope out of ear shot — 'Oh no, not again!' On the way to bed he turned to me, half serious but with a twinkle in his eye: 'Who does he think he is, flippin' Jesus?' I realise now that I shouldn't have burst into laughter — it will only make him invent even more irreverent remarks. But how accurately my boy has put his finger on things.

I wonder what sort of impression of Jesus we give to children, with our church services, school assemblies, our Bible stories and our set prayers? Jesus the goody goody? Jesus the holy holy? Jesus the killjoy? Jesus the superhuman? Jesus remote from all that is ordinary and normal? Jesus who lives in a strange sort of God-area, not in the human area? What a blasphemy. What a denial of our deepest belief that God became flesh.

I have come to believe that a very important question needs to be asked in our churches. Who best reflects the good news that Jesus preached in our world? The professional holy man with his clerical garb and his supernatural language? Or the average mum and dad, or single lay person, who have accepted Jesus' word that God is where love is, and who try to live out that teaching unobtrusively in their lives?

I know priests and nuns who do live out that teaching unobtrusively in their lives. The love they radiate is their preaching of the gospel. First among these 'Good News' nuns is my sister, Georgette. She entered the convent after me, becoming a Sister of Mercy. Today she heads the Catholic primary school in Bangor, North

Wales, and is loved and respected by all the families whom she has helped and the community she quietly and untiringly serves. But I worry about the centuries-old presumption in our church that bishops, priests and nuns know best about almost everything. I even had a priest tell me recently that he could understand Pedro better than I could because he had spent several years caring for boys in a children's home. 'And anyway,' he said, 'Pedro is not your own child, he is only adopted.' I was dumbfounded at his arrogance. And at his ignorance.

There are times now when I would dearly love to interrupt the sermon at Mass, especially when it is patently obvious that a priest is utterly remote from the experience of his congregation. Why should he be telling me what I should feel? I have enough religious background to make up my own mind, but many of the congregation are made to feel guilty. No wonder Pedro once remarked that people in church always look miserable.

One Sunday last year the priest was talking about preparing for Christmas. All our rushing about, our shopping and planning of special meals, our worries over choosing presents, our paperchains and tinsel, our frantic last-minute sending of cards — all this is worldly and not what Christmas is about, he said. Christmas, he pronounced, is about the quiet coming of Christ into the world. We can only recognise it in peace and stillness.

It was at this point in the sermon that I wanted to stand up and shout 'Objection'. It simply isn't true for me. God, in Christ, isn't only present in peace and calm. Surely the whole Christmas story is telling us that God is present everywhere and especially in the most ordinary busy events of life. Certainly, the ordinary event of the birth of a baby is not a calm experience. Ask women who have been through it. The joyful chaos of Christmas preparation in a family is exactly where God is found. I remember the quiet Christmas nights in my novitiate days. Kneeling silently before the crib in the dark chapel, lights flickering   a lovely setting for meditation. But it had nothing to do with the reality of a young mother exhausted by birth, almost frightened of the fragile baby so dependent on her. It had little to do with the experience of post-natal depression or of a father feeling excluded from this new relationship.

I remember having a very romantic idea of Mary. She is, of course, the ideal woman, the virgin, held up as the model for nuns Her motherhood is dehumanised first by insisting on the importance of her 'virginity' and secondly by transferring her mothering of Jesus to her mothering of 'the Church'. For mothers themselves Mary is also held up as a model. But the effectiveness of her example is ruined by the doctrines which surround her. I remember the occasion which forced me to analyse the position of Mary in our Catholic thinking.

Pedro, aged five and ever cheerful, was humming and singing all day. He was going through his school repertoire and, like a record stuck in a groove, he was repeating over and over again the line 'The little Lord Jesus, no crying he makes' In between the singing we had tears and quarrels Blanca was fed up with Pedro's cheerfulness. She mucked up his game of cars. I got cross. More tears. As the day wore on the idea of a perfect, non-crying baby Jesus and a composed mother Mary really annoyed me What a mother needs to know is that all children are the same and that other mums lose patience. As a Catholic mother exhorted to look to Mary as a model for motherhood, I want her, in fact I need her to have experienced the same tiredness and frustrations. It makes no sense that Jesus didn't cry as a baby. If he didn't he wasn't human. Is he really supposed never to have thrown a two-year-old tantrum? Never to have stamped a three-year-old's foot and shouted 'No'? Never to have whined and wanted his own way *now* as a four-year-old? If Mary was spared our common mother experiences of the more painful kind, I don't think she can be our example. When I walk around a supermarket and see a mother dragging an unwilling youngster round, or losing patience with an insistent 'wanting, wanting' child, I feel very close to that mum. I know exactly how tired she feels. I now presume that Mary is close to us in this same way and joins in the sense of community that I feel with all mothers. She has been there too.

The doctrine of Mary's virginity has done enormous harm to the laity in the Church. By interpreting the biblical language of virginity as a straight biological fact, the early Church Fathers raised the celibate life to a position of superiority. Marriage was necessary for some, but it was second best and rather impure. The main purpose of marriage seemed to be to provide a continued supply of celibates. What a travesty. During one of my retreats as a nun I remember feeling highly privileged that I had avoided motherhood! The spiritual director was commenting on the gospel incident where a woman shouted out to Jesus 'How happy is the woman who bore and nursed you!' Jesus replied, said Luke, with the words, 'Rather, how happy are those who hear the word of God and obey it.' The priest told us that our obedience and discipleship as religious was far more important than family relationships.

Now I understand that Jesus wasn't putting family life down, and certainly not putting his mother down. He was saying that Mary was blessed not because she was his mother but because she understood the Good News he proclaimed. And what good news it is. God is love. How happy are those who love and are loved. Nuns, priests, single lay people, married people, homosexual people — any one who loves, really loves, with all its demands and sacrifices — are the ones blessed with the truth that sets us free.

Blanca made a quaint comment on this quite recently. 'Mummy,' she said, 'can God draw hearts?' When I asked what she meant by her question, she said: 'Well, God is loving. He loves everyone and when you love, you draw hearts. Why did he make the moon round? Why didn't he make it like a heart? (pause) Perhaps he can only draw circles.' What a daughter. I'm blessed for being her mother.

That evening in Neiva, I so looked forward to meeting Sister Angelica in order to share our children with her once again. If it hadn't been for her we would never have known this joy.

9 RE-THINKING

DIARY August 9

A totally different day today, with plenty of hardship, but no real frustration.

First the meeting with Claudia Angelica. We heard she did finally arrive at 9.30 pm, while we were at the restaurant. Relief. She stayed at the hotel with the BBC. Urgent message that we should turn up at the bus station at 9.30 am. The crew would film a genuine first meeting, even though staged. To get in our swim, Blanca and I got up at 6.30 to use a family private pool up the road.

Mauricio was rather put out that his plan of meeting her at his house had been overruled by the interpreter Joyce. And he lost again when his second plan of having his whole family and brother accompany us into camera shots was also foiled by Joyce hoiking them out at the last minute.

The actual meeting at the bus station was delightful, and again highly emotional. The cameras both intruded yet didn't, our real joy and animated conversation in Spanish and German overcoming everything. We walked off with Claudia Angelica through the crowded square as if no one else existed.

The journey to La Argentina was arduous but so free from pressure that it was like going on holiday. I sat in the back of our van with Claudia Angelica and her mother Beatriz, and we never stopped talking, laughing and crying for hours on end — Bert providing the occasional translation in Deutsch or Español. The children entertained us all the way.

About an hour on a good tarmac road through a wide plain flanked by two impressive mountain ranges, green, brown, blue and purple as they receded — part of one of the Andes Cordilleras. Very lush, with grass and trees right to the summit. Then, for the hours that followed, a dirt track. Dust galore, so that we had to plead with our driver not to breathe so close down the neck of the other van, and give the dust a chance to settle. We wrote a cinquaine:

Pedro,
Back of the van,
Yawned because he was tired,
Swallowed a great mouthful of dust,
Speechless.

The road often narrowed to a cart-track, with surface to match. But this was heaven compared with the hair-raising detour we were advised to take to avoid a broken down lorry ahead, apparently blocking the already narrow road. The detour gave me the bumpiest and most precarious piece of motoring I have yet experienced. Pedro excitedly compared it to a rally course. Bert's reaction was to compose a parable: 'A certain lorry went up the road from Neiva to La Argentina. And on the way it had a breakdown. And a BBC van came by on the same road, and took a detour.' Blanca's comment: 'No wonder Jesus said it's better on a donkey.'

We rejoined the 'main road', still potholed dirt but no longer mountaineering, and stopped to stretch legs and to have a beer and a kebab in La Plata which had all the feel of a cowboy town. I expected to see Clint Eastwood turn the corner. And so to the last lap meandering up the valley. Vast perpendicular cliffs covered in moss and grass were explained to us by Pedro: 'It's the Niagara falls, only they've turned it off.'

We finally came to our first view of La Argentina nestling in a hollow in the mountains. Breathtaking. Beautiful in the early evening light. A rainbow suddenly appeared, framing the whole village. What an extraordinary welcome!

And so we finally swept triumphantly into the 'main' street, and Claudia Angelica's mother's house. Cousins, aunts, nephews galore crowded round, rather as at Mauricio's Dad's, but with a difference. This was no mere polite and formal greeting. There were pumping handshakes, embraces, kisses, introductions. Two pigs tied up in front of the house joined in. Alan, our cameraman, had jumped out of the first van to capture the spontaneous scene. The village (named La Argentina after the ancient Indian silver mines) is rather like the German hill village Bert was born in, in the 1920s: dirt roads, huddled houses, shops interspersed, everyone knowing everyone else, strangers an object of interest and welcome, children following you wherever you go. Indoors, a spacious balcony overlooking the hills for a living and eating area, kitchen galley and bedrooms off (very basic, one washing point for everyone, and an outside loo).

We were ushered in to a meal which they had expected to give us at 2.00 pm. Great dishes of rice, chicken, egg and avocado salad, with three different kinds of potato. Sumptuous, but much was sent back: in spite of nibbling only crisps on the way, the hard journey had blighted our hunger. They fed twelve of us, and then sat down to eat themselves. Crates of beer arrived, and we stood and sat on the balcony and in the tiny armchaired parlour chatting. Chatting is the wrong word. Huila people all shout in conversation, often three or four of them at the same time. The schoolmaster showed Bert the script of a speech of civic welcome which was due to have been delivered at 3.00 pm today, but has now been postponed till tomorrow. He corrected the details for them.

The weather has turned blessedly cool here in the mountains. It rained this evening to clear the air. Heaven.

It is quite wonderful to spend some days with Claudia Angelica and her family. For the past nine years we have tried to share the children with them, but letters and photographs are pitifully inadequate to convey the wonder of children's growth. A brief meeting would also be frustrating. It will take some days for Pedro to reveal his constant, infectious humour and easy nature, and for Blanca to overwhelm them by her sensitive and warm personality.

This is not the first reunion with Claudia Angelica. We spent a weekend with her in Simpelveld when the children were four. Back then she was nervous that over those four years they would have lost their spontaneous South American exuberance, and that we would have turned them into prim little Europeans. No need to worry. Pedro whooshed along the polished corridors on his bottom, spilled orange juice over the hand-embroidered parlour table cloth, played cars on the chapel floor during Mass, and broke all language barriers by his constant chatter to Sister Claudia. Blanca held Claudia's hand the whole weekend. They spoke together without knowing each other's language. Yet she asked, 'Why can't you speak English? I can, and I'm only four.' Everywhere we went she cuddled up to her, and as we left the convent she again made Claudia weep by whispering spontaneously, 'Thank you for looking after me when I was a baby.' And Pedro said his good-bye by poking his head out of the car window and shouting, 'I'm from Colombia too.'

Yes, it is good to be together again. An opportunity to recall for Sister Claudia and Beatriz many of the precious moments that Bert and I have had with the children. We have discovered that parents have so much to learn from the directness and generosity of their children. Time and again I have been brought up sharp by Blanca's vision or Pedro's profound reflection, always clearer and deeper than my own.

There was the occasion when I took Pedro and Blanca to a local school for the mentally handicapped.

We sat for a long time holding the hands of a little Asian girl, Suheila, who was the size of a toddler though already seven. Her little legs were withered and her face disfigured. She was deaf and blind and only aware of us by touch. Pedro and Blanca chatted about their morning all the way home. When I asked them to tell Daddy about their new friend Suheila, Blanca said, 'Daddy, she was just like us. She had black hair. But she was poorly.' Blanca noticed first of all what united them. I saw first of all that she was very different from my two with her distorted little face and her lifeless body. I resolved from then on to try and see things positively as Blanca did.

There are times too when Pedro shows a greater wisdom than mine. He did just this when he was three years old and I watched him, unseen, at playgroup. There was a highly disturbed boy in the group. His behaviour was destructive and negative. I had secretly hoped Pedro would keep away from him and play with the conforming children. I watched the boy playing, as usual, alone in the sand pit. Suddenly Pedro approached him, slowly. He sat near him; he moved closer; he offered him a toy truck. I watched with bated breath as the boy snatched it away. Pedro stayed there quietly and within five minutes the two of them were playing peacefully together.

It is experiences like these that have made me realise the presence of God in my ordinary, everyday life. All religious words seem unnecessary in the presence of a human experience that is illuminated by love, acceptance, forgiveness and welcome. We are always in danger of imposing holy words on a reality which is totally human and secular. I suspect that we can make life very difficult for the children in the future if we start putting 'holy' labels on their most human and instinctive responses. For God is present when love is present. If the Christian doctrine of Incarnation means anything at all it means that God is present precisely in the most secular and human events of our daily lives. He was present when Pedro approached the difficult boy. (He was present this morning when I was interrupted umpteen times by telephone calls and door bells as I tried to edit these pages.) He is present when I realise I have not defrosted the loaf I need for breakfast and when Blanca remembers (as she leaves for school) that she was supposed to take a clean PE shirt. Putting religious words on to the reality doesn't make it any more real. For young children it can be counterproductive. It can turn religion into mere magic, and so remove God into the area of the unreal, a fantasy world.

Bert and I became aware of the whole problem of religious language during the Easter celebrations in the children's first year at school. Pedro asked me one day, 'Mummy, is Jesus really alive? 'Cos if he is, why haven't we asked him round to our house?' And with a chuckle, he added, 'And I'd give him a cheese sandwich.' His quaint thinking shook me a bit. I remembered how Blanca had said one night as she got into bed, 'Goodnight Jesus and I hope you're not afraid of the Holy Ghost.' Bert asked amidst the giggles that followed, 'What's all this about the Holy Ghost? Who is it?' Quick as a flash Pedro replied, 'Well, it's certainly not me, Dad.'

What do our children understand of the God-language that trips so easily off our tongues? We became even more aware of a problem when first communion came on the horizon. Children offer logical answers to their own theological questions. Why, then, start to prepare children for their first communion at the very age when their imaginations are most wild and wonderful?

One evening, when Blanca was six, she told me a story before she went to bed. (We were taking it in turns to tell the bedtime story.)

> Mummy, what do you think of this? Supposing you turned into a biscuit or bread; no, into an apple pie. And somebody ate you up. Then you suddenly turned back into you. And that very big, enormous person you were inside, suddenly ate a strawberry, but you were struggling to get out, so he bit your fingers and your toes.

Blanca fell about laughing at her own story and I laughed with her. I asked her whatever made her think of such a strange thing. But I had a rather uneasy suspicion. Two minutes earlier Pedro had vaguely mentioned Jesus as he recounted some of the things they had been hearing in the assembly. The older children were preparing for first communion and I could well imagine that some of this preparation had spilled over into the celebrations that the younger children attended. Was Blanca's story the result of a six-year-old's imagination trying to make sense of the notion of 'receiving Jesus' in communion in the form of bread?

Another day Blanca announced that they had had Mass in the hall instead of assembly. Pedro interrupted her. 'Mummy, Matthew said that Father Tony had blood in the cup. He wouldn't drink that would he? Yuk!' Their teacher then told me that one child had asked if communion will taste like meat, 'because you are eating a body'.

It seems strange to me now that children receive their first communion at this age of heightened imagination. Strange, that is, only if we insist on presenting the sacrament as 'receiving the body of Jesus in communion'.

This is the age when children recite by heart the story of Red Riding Hood and the Gingerbread Man — stories where people are gobbled up. This is the age when they are captivated by dinosaurs eating the flesh of other dinosaurs, and when cannibal stories are an awesome revelation.

We decided to prepare our two for communion by simply talking about remembering Jesus as we share bread and wine. We have good gospel backing for this. We concentrated on John's account of the Last Supper, where Jesus talks about loving and serving one another, with no mention of the bread 'being' his body. Children have a natural concern for others so it is a wonderful opportunity to harness their generosity — not least to learn from it for ourselves.

About this time I learnt from my daughter to act upon any generous impulse. It was 6.30 pm and the children were bathed and ready for bed. With an extraordinary air of insistence Blanca announced, 'Mummy, before we go to bed I want to take Michael a toy.' I pointed out that it wasn't a very good idea to go down the road in pyjamas, so we would go in the morning. 'No, Mummy, I want to go *now*.' Something in her determined face spoke to me. We put coats and shoes on. Michael was a young neighbour's nine-month-old son. He was dying from a brain tumour. Christine had brought him home from hospital to die, only a week earlier. We sat with this sad, single mother for half an hour, Blanca gazing gently at the unconscious baby and holding out her monkey for him. Pedro gave him a car and then chatted quietly to Christine about what he had done at school. At 3 am our door bell rang. It was Christine. Could she use our phone? The baby had died.

There are always wonderful opportunities for families

to explore generosity and service to others. Of course, it can be quite demanding! There was the barbecue day, for example, the first time we used the set given us at Christmas. On the first warm day of the year as Bert unpacked it and set it up in the garden, disaster. The doorbell rang. Three next-door children trooped in at Blanca's invitation. We already had three other children to lunch and Bert was worn out entertaining them. He barked at them that we were busy. But their father followed. Could the childen see the new barbecue being set on fire? Shamefaced, Bert offered him some home-made wine. Slowly the sausages frizzled. Blanca counted them and announced, 'Dad, there are ten sausages, and only eight of us. They could stay for tea too.' Three pairs of eyes lit up. So half an hour later all eight children were eating sausages. Blanca's spontaneous generosity had once more put our selfish interests to shame.

Of course, Blanca had not yet realised that generosity costs. Towards the end of the proceeding, she wailfully announced that she'd only had one and a half sausages, and why weren't there any more? Pedro still had half of one left. 'Here you are Blanca,' he said. 'I've had enough.'

I was once invited to write an article about religious language for a Catholic publication. I decided to explore this idea of concentrating upon children's generosity as an introduction to first communion, using John's gospel as inspiration. The editor declined to publish what I had written because 'it raises so many questions'. He insisted that it would distort the truth if children weren't given the whole (adult) doctrine of transubstantiation.

Another point he feared would raise too many awkward questions was my suggestion about 'sin' language.

I have always argued that 'sin' seems too fierce a word to apply to young children. When the time came for Pedro and Blanca to prepare for their first confession (the Church still demands that children receive the sacrament of Reconciliation, or confession, before they receive communion), I began to be uncertain whether this Catholic practice was going to be very helpful. I was not impressed when the priest at our first confession/communion parent meeting tried to convince us that seven year olds are quite capable of committing SIN. (He emphasised the word.) By sin he meant a deliberate '*no*' to God. I reminded him that even Herbert McCabe's *New Catechism* makes no mention of childish naughty behaviour in the chapter on Penance. The sacrament, for him, is a 'welcoming back from grave sin'. That surely is applicable only to adults.

Children know how to disturb the peace and try adult patience. That isn't sin. I remember once a tiring day when the children were in high spirits and constantly arguing. I finally snapped. Blanca was leaping round the bathroom, waving her nightdress in the air. It finally dropped in the bath. I was cross and shouted at her. It went very quiet and a minute later I found her sitting on her bed weeping. She sobbed, 'Mummy, why are you being so unkind to me?' I felt very bad. I knew that she was right, and yet even then, I was so wrapped up in my own tiredness that I couldn't respond instantly with a cuddle. I just snapped, 'Because I'm tired and you're being silly.'

In fact the poor little girl wasn't being naughty. (I expect that priest would want her to confess to being thoughtless and unhelpful to her Mummy.) I should be grateful for her good humour and energy. She didn't throw her nightdress into the bath deliberately. Later I was so sad that she saw my unreasonable bad-temper as unkindness. And I 'let the sun go down on my anger', a thing I vowed never to do. She cried herself quietly to sleep, and I spent one miserable night of regret. In the morning I was able to say sorry, and Blanca hugged me and said, 'Oh Mummy, that's alright. I love you.'

What more has the sacrament of Reconciliation to offer than this exchange of love, forgiveness and understanding that Blanca and I experienced? I know and feel the forgiveness and love of God for me in my daughter's forgiveness and love. I don't see that I had anything to forgive Blanca for.

We celebrate as a family God's forgiving love over and over again. All families do. I celebrated it the night three-year-old Pedro brought a lump to my throat when I kissed him good-night. I whispered, 'I love you Pedro, such a lot.' He whispered back, 'But do you love me when I'm naughty?' (He had just tipped a whole bottle of bubble bath down the toilet.) I hugged him tight and told him that I loved him all the time, even when he was naughty. 'I don't like the naughty things you sometimes do, but you, Ped, I love the whole time', I said. He stroked my cheek and said, 'Oh, that's nice.'

My Catholic editor also insisted that children commit sin — 'What about their cruelty to one another and to their parents?' he asked. Children who are shouted at learn to shout. Children who are hit learn to hit out at other children. Children who are cruel have learnt it from adults. I would want to pin the sin on to the adults. We learn as parents how to avoid getting our children into situations which force them to behave badly.

I once made a big mistake. I shouted out from the kitchen, in an accusing voice, 'Who spilt the milk?' 'She did,' shouted Pedro. 'He did,' shouted Blanca. The Adam and Eve syndrome I call it. A definite case of lying my priest would call it. One of them had to be telling an untruth! But I was actually the one at fault. I was far too threatening in my manner. Had I calmly said, 'Hello, the milk has got spilt. Will one of you come and help me clear it up?' I would have got a positive response and an accurate explanation of the accident.

So I've learnt a lot from my children. So have all parents. The actual experience of bringing up children is an education in itself. The pity is that this education is hardly ever given any credit. We parents do a lot of listening to the experience of the unmarried — it comes over us like a waterfall from every pulpit. But if they are the official spokesmen for the Church (that is to say, for *us*), ought they not, at least occasionally, to *listen* to us?

We were recently at a friend's wedding. And the nonsense of the situation swept over me. In spite of the recognition that the sacrament of marriage is a solemn contract made between a man and a woman who love each other, it is heavily dominated by the words of the unmarried priest — especially in his sermon. He presumes the right to tell the couple the meaning of their marriage and the way to live it. I wonder how many married couples the priest actually listens to before he dares to speak.

In this instance the priest was a kind, sensible young man, obviously appreciated by many. Yet his words were transparently unreal. How could they be otherwise? He had chosen *not* to get married. He told us that the marriage would only last if Anne had chosen Peter solely because she wanted to make him happy; and if Peter had chosen Anne solely to make her happy. If they were after any happiness for themselves it was a recipe for divorce. That kind of exhortation to heroic, selfless love is enough to inspire lifelong guilt. It is typical of holy sermons and little related to the needs of human beings. Anne and Peter need to choose happiness for themselves too.

I'm not demanding that *only* parents can tell the Church about the bringing up of children. But at least parents ought to be listened to. At least they ought not to be slapped down every time they raise their voice. Parents are closest to their children. They know what children are capable of, and what they are not. Yet we continue to be told by 'experts' — almost exclusively male and celibate — (bishops, priests, theologians, textbooks) how we are to pass on our faith to our children. Why can't we be trusted? Why can't we be taken seriously?

I shared many of these stories with Sister Claudia Angelica, though I can't pretend that I discussed with her all the reflections to which they have given rise in my mind. For all her openness, my revolutionary thoughts might have shocked her. But at least she *listens*. She listens most acutely when she becomes totally poor with her poor people, and teaches three school-shifts everyday, from 7.00 in the morning until 10.00 at night. Unmarried as she is, does *she* know her fellow Christians! Does *she* know what liberation the gospel can bring to the afflicted!

I can't help contrasting the image of the Church at the back of her mind with the one recently issued to us in our English diocese. An official publication solemnly showed us this structure (see the page opposite):

The laity are crushed by the weight of the professionals. Our voices are bound to be unheard. We are down in the basement.

Such a top-heavy Church must eventually topple over. In our weary North, it is at present showing every sign of cracking up. Here in the South I am discovering a more people-centred Church, a Church in which

POSSIBLE DIOCESAN STRUCTURE SHOWING RELATIONSHIPS

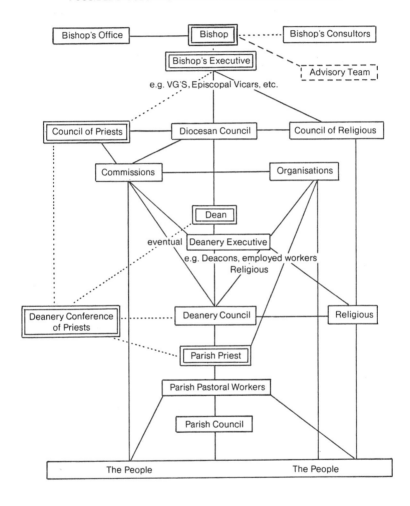

Jesus the poor layman can feel at home, a Church in which the gospel continues to be seen for the good news it is.

I thank God that because of Sister Claudia Angelica, I have come here with Blanca and Pedro to share something of their heritage and to be reconfirmed in my hopes for the future.

10 FULL CIRCLE

DIARY August 10

Some of our friends doubted the wisdom of this journey
to La Argentina. They feared that the villagers would be
embarrassed, even aggressive, or that Pedro and Blanca
would be upset and confused. I wish they had been with
us today. We have found in the children's village a
warmth and a welcome that has surpassed anything we
had hoped for.

Our neighbour's hourly 'cock-a-clock' finally got us up
at 7.00. Cups of black, home-grown coffee waited for us.
Then breakfast for everyone, BBC crew included (they
had lodged with families up the road), at 7.30. Scrambled
eggs, toast, butter and jam.

Then a leisurely walk down town, stopped all the way
by people who are part of the children's history — Mario
who went up the hill with Sister Claudia Angelica to
bring the children down; Mercedes the former mayor's
mother who first received them into her house, her
daughter Noelia, unmarried, who is so full of our story
that she has just adopted an eight-month-old orphan girl;
the woman who gave the children their first wash; various
nephews and nieces of the stepfather Camilo; and even
(what a surprise!) two of his sons aged 20 or so,
stepbrothers of Pedro and Blanca, grinning from ear to
ear without a trace of embarrassment. Their names,
Bertulfo and Guilberto. Cowboys galloping through
sporadically, raising the dust on the unmade roads. Down
to the Sunday Market to inspect what was on offer.
Blanca bought a rainbow hair-slide, and Pedro his first
boy scout's knife, pseudo-Swiss, made in China, only £2.

The children of the village followed us as if we were Pied Pipers.

The 10 o'clock Mass was delayed for half an hour because of a multiple baptism (nobody seemed surprised, nobody minded the delay), but was worth waiting for. A fine priest, speaking from the heart to a full church. A dog was peacefully asleep in the aisle throughout the Mass. Children strolled in and out, some sitting for a while on the floor and then leaving to play on the steps outside. Pedro stood at the side with his new friend Juan Alberto, Claudia Angelica's nephew. No musical instruments, but much popular singing throughout the service. The sense of a community happy with their faith and happy with one another. The priest, referring to today's gospel, the Transfiguration of Christ, touched on the theme: 'Where is God present or absent in our lives?' One thing was certain. He is present in the quiet, patient dignity of these impoverished *campesinos* — country people. Starry-eyed, I have to jerk myself to remember that he is also present in my middle-class, rather anonymous cathedral parish at home in England.

The greatest surprise of this whole journey has been the willingness, indeed the anxiety of the stepfather Camilo to establish contact with us. Our BBC producer met him a month ago when he visited to prepare for the filming. Dick assured us that the family were anxious to welcome Pedro and Blanca 'home' to their village. We had returned to England nine years ago with only a half understood version of the children's early months. We cast Camilo into the role of wicked step-father. We had understood that he had abandoned the babies and refused to care for them even though his wife, their mother, remained in hospital for many months. It was left to four-year-old Maricela, their step-sister, to feed them.

Today we have been put right and humbled by the truth of the real story. We discovered Camilo Cabezas to be a quiet, humble, dignified, wizened little man, delighted to welcome us to his tiny farm, half an hour by jeep outside the village. He has been growing bananas, sugar, coffee and pineapples there for the last thirty years. An adequate livelihood one would imagine now, but nine years ago he reached near destitution. Delfina, mother of his six children, needed an emergency Caesarian operation to bring her twins into the world. Pedro and Blanca's father disappeared from the scene, leaving Camilo to sell up half of his land to pay the hospital fees. The operation went wrong, puncturing her bladder and leaving her critically ill for months. How could he cope with the new-born twins under these conditions? We *needed* to meet Camilo for a reconciliation. We had so badly misjudged him.

The journey up the hillside was quite an adventure. The path had to negotiate a landslide from earlier this year, and eventually to cross a ferocious torrent. A slow meander over rocky ground through a jungle of banana and coffee groves. Then the path ended. We had to walk the last fifty yards further up the hillside to the freshly whitewashed house, where the lonely man was waiting for us, holding the hand of his youngest daugher, Maricela. She was aged about thirteen, very pretty, but tiny, and with a close resemblance to Blanca. This was the girl who, herself still a tot, had mothered the sickly twins nine years ago. Blanca had been yearning over the years for this moment.

The meeting was dignified and warm, not effusive as the others had been. Yet because of the circumstances, strangely moving. We were led into the house, to be shown the tiny room where the twins had lived their few months there. Primitive to the extreme, yet with a certain dignity. No toilets at all — the field outside made do.

Lunch was miraculously produced by aunts hidden in the background and working from a kitchen range which resembled one of our cheaper garden barbecue sets. A tasty meal of chicken, rice, soup, potatoes, cooked bananas — eaten in relays and served on plates the BBC had provided for the family.

Many photographs recorded our visit. Camilo and his children were anxious to be filmed with us. They showed a pride in Pedro and Blanca, perhaps recognising that their quiet grace is a Colombian heritage. For much of the visit Pedro played happily with Juan Alberto amongst the palms and tropical vegetation. Earlier, down in the village, Pedro and Blanca had become a little fed up by being such a centre of attention. But up here, on their mountainside, they were happy to be with just a few children. They took Bert's advice and answered in English when they were addressed in Spanish. It worked well. Blanca stayed beside Maricela most of the time. Although thirteen years old she is six inches shorter than Blanca at nine. Malnutrition? Yet she is extraordinarily beautiful, with a quiet grace and a most charming smile. At another time, as she sat with Sister Claudia in her tiny, bare bedroom (all her possessions fit on one small shelf), she told her with tears that this was the happiest day of her life.

We had to take our leave — we will meet up again tomorrow in the village — to attend some receptions. First at the house of Mercedes, with apple champagne and delicious crispy maize fries. Then a dash to the village centre to the Municipal Council Chamber (a room upstairs over a shop) for a more formal reception by the Mayor, Chief of Police, Headmaster, Council members, and twenty or so interested people. As the speeches started Camilo quietly slipped in at the back.

A strange experience to see such an impoverished village insisting on such dignified formality out of sheer respect for human nature, and out of genuine love for two children who will never be forgotten by them. Four very fulsome speeches. An actor performed in mime the plight of the *campesinos*. Then we were presented with a 'parchment', handwritten in gold, conferring on us in perpetuity the honour of respected guests in this little town. Bert replied in his broken Spanish, to the effect that being parents of these Huila children had made us honorary *Huilenses,* and swearing the undying fellowship of La Argentina and Norwich. We made a note that we must tell our Mayor when we get back. Then we all solemnly drank champagne.

The last visit of the day was to the cemetery to pray at
the grave of Pedro and Blanca's mother, Delfina Vidal,
who died August 21 1984. We asked the BBC to be as
discreet as possible, so as not to intrude on possibly the
most sensitive moment of our pilgrimage. So they filmed
from a distance, and left us — the family and Claudia
Angelica — to say our prayers at the pitifully poor grave,
kept neat but, in contrast with far more ostentatious
graves, marked only with a black wooden cross and the
name. We put there the bunch of wild flowers that the
children had picked for us earlier, and the two silk roses
we had brought from England, one white for Blanca, and
a red one from Pedro. 'Why a red one, Mum?' Pedro
whispered. 'Perhaps for Liverpool?' A pause, then, 'No, I
know, Mum. The red one is for Death, and white one for
Life.'

We sang a soft *Requiem Aeternam*. We talked quietly
with the children about their first Mummy — that she
was now held in God's love. That whenever we love we
are close to God, and so we can be close to her too.

I came to the end of my journey at that little cemetery
on the hillside of the beautiful valley that is La Argentina. Everything in my life seemed present and held
together and complete. Sister Claudia Angelica was
there, close and prayerful and part of my nun life. Bert
was there, strong and loving as husband and father.
Pedro and Blanca were at my side and near their first
Mummy too. We had talked so often about her, and I
had always longed to bring them back and say 'Thank
you' for the most precious gift of motherhood Delfina
had shared with me.

In the quiet moments at the graveside I showed
Delfina her little Pedro who has the insight to see life
out of death in the symbol of the roses we brought to
her. I showed her the tender Blanca who had written me

103

a little note expressing her concern that I might feel sad because she was so excited at coming to find her first Mummy. 'You are both my Mummy', she wrote.

In the quiet moments at the graveside I realised how much Blanca and Pedro have taught me about walking before God in the present moment, the ideal I set out to realise by becoming a nun. I have come full circle. I have come home.